The Real Fake World

By Daniel Lebost

CHAPTER ONE

People have this problem with always trying to reach higher than they should ever go. This thought keeps going through my head as I stare out the window of a commercial jet, a good 39,000 feet above the Atlantic Ocean. I think about how much it would suck to take a nose dive right into it. At the same time, I can't help but notice how beautiful it is up here and how I've managed to get this far; I guess how humanity has ever gotten this far. The light blue sky, the white puffy clouds, a bright sun and all that cockamamie bullshit are reflecting perfectly off the wing. It is perfect. It's all perfect and all so amazingly beautiful.

When I was a kid, I used to lay down with my back on the ground and my eyes would focus in on the clouds. I would try to make specific shapes out of them. I could make them into anything: bears, dragons, lions, different peoples faces, pirate ships. It was all so innocently imagined. If they moved a slight bit they could change into something completely different. Just in a single instant they could go from a dinosaur to a cat. One single instant was all that it took— it is all that it takes. Now I am physically in the clouds, I am in the dream, I am in the imagination, and all it takes is an instant.

I look forward at one of the television monitors set a few seats in front of me showing all the pretty pictures, and I know those pictures well. I see them all the time. It's a show about people with happy lives and meaningless drama in between where there's lots of laughing and very little crying. It's just how it should be.

I hear a rustling noise throughout the cabin and the captain gives a low cough to clear his throat. He speaks over the intercom. Before the words even come out of his mouth I know he's delivering bad news or the flight attendant would have reported the message.

"Ladies and gentleman, it is at this time that I would like to ask everyone who is not in their seats to get to them as quickly as possible. We are about to run into some turbulence and it is for your own safety that everyone place their tray tables in the upright position and to please buckle in your—".

He doesn't even get to finish the sentence.

There's a loud rip and tear drowning out the sound coming from the intercom and suddenly all the lights start flickering on and off and all the little beeps and alarms echo off one another all at once. Everyone is turning their heads in different directions trying to sense what is going on. A few gasps, but no screams. Not yet. They can't scream yet.

It's the shock.

It's the shock.

She's dead.

It's the shock.

From dinosaur to cat.

From being there to being nothing at all.

One second.

I can see it though. The wing out my passenger window is partially torn off and I'm waiting for the rest to go with it.

I know it will.

I can see it before it even happens, but I don't want to.

I keep telling myself this is not real, this is not possible, this cannot happen. There is a white mist shooting past us and I can smell gasoline. We're gaining speed and I'm still as calm as a Zen Buddhist just watching it all go down, getting ready. Watching.

The seat in front of me is a mixture of blue and red dots gone completely haywire in a psychedelic hallucination. Then it comes. A loud crack like the largest tree on the face of the earth twenty feet away just got struck by lightening and snapped right in half. There's no time to react and there's nothing to fall back on. It's the shock. It's pain and anguish and screaming in one instant going right through my spine, through everyone's spine. The tree of life, your life, SNAP. All in one instant.

The wing has broken off and waves of pure panic erupt through the entire cabin and now the screaming starts. The beeps feel like little shocks of electricity throughout each one of my nerve endings and my blood begins to boil and my stomach lifts up and hangs weightlessly in the air. All of my food is brought right to the back end of my throat. My heart is beating louder than all the little beeps and the screams of nearby children combined. I hear them screaming like they're far, far away. Or maybe it's just me screaming.

This one instant takes away all the beauty you have ever known. Forget all of your experiences, all the sex, all the love you have ever given or received. Forget drugs and all the kind things you have ever done for anyone because in that one-second you would take it all back and kill them all just to make it stop. Kill everyone just make it stop. PLEASE!

Somebody shut that kid up. Shut that fucking kid up! Tell him to be a man and suck it up and accept it. Tell him to absorb the fear, take it all in and breathe the plague of hell deep into his heart. Suck it up and take it. Breathe, just breathe.

My mind turns to all the Yogi and Buddhist crap I've ever learned. Just breathe. My mind goes to all of my therapy sessions. Just release and let go. My mind tries to think about the Tao and the Buddhist teachings: just be and let be, listen to the Tao. Do not try and control, simply walk where your legs will take you and do not try and guide them and you will be all right.

Well, forget all of that because right now, in this moment, in this very instant, nothing can control instinct. No mindset can prevent me from that fall. No Buddhist, no yogi, no amount of therapy, and no amount drugs or tears will let me hold that plane up with my mind. Instinct takes over and my senses bow down on both knees to its will. You can't breathe with no oxygen. The elements have taken over. All the beauty is undone in one single moment. Why did we ever climb so high so we could fall so far? If we had never left the ground we would still be lying on it staring up at the clouds. I would still be that little kid lying on my back with my eyes to the sky, dreaming and imagining. Imagination could never hurt as much as this.

The plane's nose tips at an angle from the wing breaking. It doesn't even do me the common decency of going down straight, it has to go down at a goddamn angle. We tumble downward into a full out spin, but I feel the pilot trying to pull us back and I'm so disoriented that my body and mind have no comprehension of what is happening. I can't even see the water, but I know the plane is taking a 700 mph nose dive at an angle right towards it. All that cockamamie bull shit about getting the oxygen masks and the life rafts and the stupid exit plans are all beyond thought, beyond reason, beyond comprehension, beyond math, beyond science, beyond everything. And most importantly beyond your arms reach because I'm spiraling downward at a goddamn angle.

The one engine left is roaring louder than the loudest demon and my scariest nightmare. This is my scariest nightmare. It is no dream. I'm going down and I'm going down harder than I could have ever fallen. If only I hadn't reached so high. If only I hadn't loved her so much.

But I'm completely fine.

There is no rip or tear and the plane is not crashing. All I'm doing is staring at the ocean thinking about her and our plane is on a steady course back home to New York. Despite it all, I look out the window and I can't help to think how beautiful it is up here.

CHAPTER TWO

My mom is dying. I know she is because they, you know, the experts, the doctors told me so. They dress in white robes and wear circular glasses because they can't look at you directly without hiding behind those damn glasses. They have slight indents in their cheeks from giving so much bad news to good people and everyone hating them for it. Their greatest sign of emotion is when they stop and sit down, but they don't say anything for a few seconds: that's when you know things are at their worst. The captain is speaking, my mom is dying, and we're spiraling down at a goddamn angle.

My friend Connor is the first person I tell. He's the only person I tell for awhile. He asks me if something is wrong and he doesn't wait for my response and he says he knows something is wrong. I hate him and love him for being one of the few people who can read between the lines of my act, my fakeness, and know that something is definitely wrong.

I smile.

"No, nothing is wrong," is my one last attempt.

"No," he says, staring straight into my eyes as he shakes his head. "You're lying. What's wrong?"

Bastard. My smile disappears and I can't lie to him anymore. At least not while he's staring me in the eyes. You have to really care in order to stare someone straight in the eyes and Connor doesn't wear glasses.

I hesitate for a moment, trying to decide the best way to tell him. How can I tell him what I can't even tell myself? But I can trust him. I have to trust someone because from my perspective the world is making less and less sense. It is destroying itself and I can only watch it happen.

"Can we take a walk?"

He nods his head and says sure and we walk out the front door of the dormitory.

I love Connor, but I also hate him. Why is this always the case with the people you're closest with? Connor is like me or maybe I would like to believe he is except he's better looking and has blue eyes. He has blonde hair and I have black. He has blue eyes and I have green. The world I have known for so long separates into these dichotomies I have no control over. The slightest differences like eye color and hair can, in the end, tear two people apart. Maybe one can talk better too, while the other is more reflective and a better listener. The differences get more and more spread out too: one of us may use Pantene Pro-V body wash and the other Axe. Maybe one comes in an off white bottle and the other marine blue. Their shapes can be different too, with one being a little wider and a top that rounds out and the other being thinner and the top conforming more subtly to its body. People can notice the slightest differences without consciously knowing it. Maybe I wouldn't hate Conner as much if somebody would only take a second look into green eyes instead of immediately loving blue. But I'm a hypocrite because I'm a sucker for blue eyes. Similarities can tear people apart too: Connor and I both like the same women.

I knew I loved women, like really loved women, since I was five-years-old and my baby sitter took me into the women's locker room to change into our swimsuits. We went into a red stall, one with those cement floors that have a slimy bottom texture from stagnant water. I watched as she took off her clothes casually like I wasn't even there, but she soon noticed that I was admiring her rather than being oblivious and this made her uncomfortable. She asked me to wait outside. I don't know what happened. Maybe my dick went hard or something and I didn't even notice because you don't notice those kinds of things when you're five-years-old, but somehow I noticed her. She must have looked into my dark green eyes and seen that there was far more going on behind them than any five-year-old kid should have. But how can you not notice the curves of a body so intricately formed, so sculpted, yet so delicate? Her pale skin looked magical from the small bits of light that shined on her through the cracks of the red box. It was like Christmas watching her unique body unfold in front of me. I could only speculate the reasons for clothing at all was to hide something so beautiful and prevent us from doing nothing but admire it all the time. I wanted to touch everything. At five-years-old, nobody had to spell this stuff out for me.

If you couldn't guess, Connor is the talkative one with the Pantene Pro-V body wash and he also knows exactly who he is. He knows what to say and when to say it and his parents and sister are all healthy; perfectly goddamn healthy and I'm happy for him— him and his goddamn perfect healthy family. Connor knows what he likes and he likes cars. It's simple. Everything for him is simple. There is no, 'maybe I'll work on a bicycle today'. No, he likes to work on just cars, fine tune and perfect them. He wants them to sound nice and if his car were to ever get scratched it would send him into an uncontrollable rage. He would do anything for that car.

I don't know about any of that. My car is old and worn down and I love every scratch on it. I use it like it's a bumper car and used to drive it through the town backwards just for kicks. My friends and I would scream out the windows, yelling about how drunk we were even though we weren't.

We knew we were drunk on something though. Maybe it was freedom. Maybe we were drunk with the antidote for all the hypocrisy we saw in the world and we healed ourselves with a dose of pure insanity. It was wonderful.

I drove carefully and slow. I stopped at every stop sign and drove on the correct side of the road – just backwards. Is that so bad? But if you could have seen the looks we got! We imagined what would have happened had we gotten pulled over. "What seems to be the problem officer? I know I wasn't speeding?"

Those looks are carved in my mind so distinctly because they were the faces of horror as if we were devils sent from hell. What did we do exactly to warrant that? It is as if we were sent to disrupt all the order in the world and maybe we were. Maybe I am. Maybe that's what dark green eyes are for.

Connor knows what he likes and he likes cars. I guess I just love everything, even driving backwards, and every little scratch because it represents a time in my life that I existed. My car lives and breathes. It gets hurt and it remembers. Should I want to cover all of that up? Maybe some things, but not everything.

The dichotomies continue: I reach for the stars, while Connor likes to keep his feet on the ground. Women prefer this about Connor. Women don't like darkness, they don't like pain, they do not like suffering and they do not like death— they do not like scratches in a car. I don't blame them though, and they know this is what they will find in dark green eyes, black hair, axe body wash, and someone who is better at listening than talking. I like the aesthetics of a woman, but I also like every birthmark in an odd place, every tattoo, and every scar. When I noticed my baby sitter in the locker room, I was trying to find what made me so attracted to *her* and her alone. Was it her pale skin tone and disjointed freckles over her cheeks? Was it her dirty brown hair full of curls or how smooth her skin was from her ribs to her hipbone? Oh that hipbone...The one with the purple flower tattoo and the wandering stem. How it playfully trailed lower down her body, tracing the steps your eyes should take, begging you to follow it...And I did follow it.

Imagination. You can get lost in it, but is it really *safe?* I wanted to go further. I wanted to see where the end to every trail would lead. I fly on this plane way above the ground with my head in the clouds full of imagination, looking at everything that is beautiful— watching it all, taking it all in, but this way of life takes the fall along with everything else. Scratches can be painful. Connor could keep his perfect car, his patience for a life that he thought was never going to end, and he could keep it all clean and beautiful – but I wanted to drive.

There's a choice. There is the Real and there is the Fake. You know the fake when you see it. It's the redundancy. The copy of a copy. You play into it and at some point you may start to wonder why you ever did, and maybe even why you still do. There is always a choice and I chose to see more and as a result you feel like you spend your whole life alone. You get sick of the redundancy and then people get sick of you. You could say my mom forced me to see more. I could blame her for all of this. Just as I am reaching out to Connor, to you – my blank page, my patient listener – she reached out to me. She was probably tired of being alone.

You don't understand this yet, but you will. Her imagination is different, and it brought me to heights and depths that should never be reached, especially not while you're alive.

Connor and I silently walk through the quad of the college. It's nighttime and a few lampposts guide our way down a stone path. I think about where the best place would be to tell him.

We pass by the Psychology building. It was finished only a couple of years back and rumor had it that a construction worker had died onsite. He was standing on a ladder when someone accidentally dropped a buzz saw. It swung down like a pendulum and took the guys head clean off. The person telling me at the time chuckles to himself.

"Isn't that horrible." He has a big grin on his face.

"Yeah," I look down at the stone pathway away from the kid's eyes "that really sucks." I smile a little myself because I can't help but think how nice it must be to have a quick clean death. One moment you're smiling and having a good time while breathing in fresh oxygen, enjoying the sun, and working on a building that will supply an educational foundation for the future generations of college students. Maybe he just had a child with his beautiful wife at home and while he's hammering in a nail he's thinking about them. He's thinking about them and he smiles, and at that exact moment that he smiles the saw comes right on through. Clean and through. Nothing else, just black…death.

I can't help to think how nice that must be. I know the kid who told me the story is scared even of the quick clean death, which is why he laughed. Well I'm scared too, but I know how much worse it can be or maybe we're both too young to know anything.

Connor and I pass the library and then the church. We arrive at a small courtyard and I hear a soft rustling sound. Above us is a large tulip poplar with the moonlight scattering through the leaves. I remember that tree. In one large wave it all comes back and I know this is it. This is where I'm meant to tell him. I have barely opened my mouth to speak when Connor says, "How about here?"

I'm silent.

It's the shock.

Inside I smile the biggest smile, "yeah" I say, as I look up at

the tree again,

"Here is good."

When I was first looking for a college, McDaniel ranked number three on the list. I was looking for a small school that participated in sports at the division three level. I had been swimming my whole life and enjoyed the sport, but did not want it to consume my life. I figured a division three school would be a more relaxed environment. I also wanted a school that was south from me because

I hate the cold, but one that wasn't too far south because I didn't want to be far away from home.

Home is in the suburbs of New York about a twenty-minute drive outside the City. Home is where my past lingers and I couldn't stay in a place that represents harsh reality and go to college that represents what I like to call, "The Real Fake World". College doesn't prepare you for cancer, it sets you up to be distant, to know how to think instead of how to feel. Organize your time, learn, so you can make money, have kids, and enjoy a little bit of happiness in between, then die. The real world isn't like that at all, but then again I can't tell you that because you won't understand. I can only try and describe to you the dark side of the moon and maybe after this book is done you may not even have to know what it looks like because you will be able to *feel* what it looks like.

McDaniel College was ranked number three in my oddly scaled ranking system behind Washington and Hood colleges. My parents unknowingly created this ranking system by advertising Hood and Washington with their statistics: Hood College had an undergraduate student body consisting of 80% women, Washington had 60% and McDaniel came in at about 50/50. Thus my ranking system was born.

Once on the McDaniel campus though, my opinion rapidly changed. Other than the sight of the girls who laid out on towels in nothing but bathing suits, my sentiments were more encouraged by the people who seemed relaxed, honest, and genuinely nice. When visiting Hood I found that the 80% enrollment of females was due to the overwhelming lesbian population, but in all fairness, the buildings were also old and ugly.

Forget all the stats. Forget the beauty of the campus, forget the people and for one second try to forget everything you know, and just feel. Feel the way a human being would feel before commercials and cable TV, before the news, before Internet, before electronic music, before video games, and before language ever evolved. See if you can drown out every possible sound in your head and simply listen and feel— this is how you should choose a college— like you've been there a thousand times before, like it's your oldest friend and you're meeting for the first time. My mother and I were waiting for this. To see it, feel it, know it or whatever you want to call it. A "shift" meets the best description. It's what tells me that this is the place where I'm going to be for the next four years of my life and where I'll have countless memories and experiences. If you can't tell that, then you haven't seen the real world and you have felt very little. This isn't to make you angry or upset or frustrated. It's never too late as long as you're alive.

It's like that moment before a rainstorm hits. You can be going around your usual day, doing everything normally, and maybe you haven't even checked the weather forecast, when you look up without any understanding why and you notice a silence that wasn't there before. You can feel the mist and the energy surge in the air around you and you just know in your mind, in your gut, or whatever you want to call it – that a storm is coming. Everyone has felt it. It depends on if you recognize it or not or more importantly *believe* in it.

On the tour given by a tall woman with brown hair, suddenly my focus falls off of her with no logical understanding of why. In that moment, everything she says becomes meaningless and the storm is the next four years of my life. My eyes seem to move on their own and gaze into the leaves of the overhanging tulip poplar. The wind shuffles through, whispering with a thousand voices as it passes. Voices that carry in their tones the distant journey of everywhere they have been and echoes into everywhere it will go. The light, alive and warm, shimmers through the branches. The world seems to come together, and all at once…I know. What's more amazing is that my mom, who was walking several feet ahead of me, has turned around from the tour completely on her own and as my eyes lower from the tree, so do hers. We look into each other's eyes and smile.

"Yeah Connor," I say to him. "Here is good."

It's been two and a half years since that day with my mother, but the tree still looks the same and I can almost see her the way she used to be. I close my eyes, trying to bring that moment back. Connor and I sit down on a wooden bench. A long silence ensues before I hear myself take a deep breath, "Connor," –another long pause— "my mom's dying."

Connor had heard about my mom's illness before. The whole swim team had heard about it and if it was up to me, none of them would have ever heard a fucking whisper about it. College is the real fake world. People aren't supposed to know things about you.

It was the year before, only a week before my mom was going to have major surgery. It was for the removal of an 8mm tumor in her ovaries and its outcome would determine whether or not she would live or die. At the time, I told my girlfriend this, the one thing I could barely tell myself. Her response was silence followed by, "Uh, yeah, Drew, I think we should break up." There's much more behind that, but I guess that was when she felt it would be the best time. Not that I blame her.

My father told my coach about the surgery without asking me if it would be all right. Her name is Kat.

"Your dad told me about your mom's surgery next week," Kat says, after I climb out of the pool.

Picture a nineteen-year-old boy, cold after a long practice, standing on a pool deck in nothing but a skintight black swimsuit made of Lycra. Then picture his coach bringing up his mother who could potentially die in the next week and doing so in front of all of his swim team friends who are suddenly paying close attention to the conversation.

Kat is a short woman with a haircut like Darth Vader's helmet except it is light brown. I don't even think she styles it, it just naturally falls that way. I watch as some of the other members of the swim team make their way out of the water, dragging their swim gear along with the droplets that fall behind them. They stare at the coach and I, and try and interpret what's going on. This entire moment has slowed down because I can't believe it's even happening and my eyes finally return back to Kat. All my focus goes to her, my green eyes narrow with the intent to pierce her very life and rage takes over the fact that others are around us. I keep glaring, letting her know her King's in check, edging her on to say one more goddamn word. Choose your next words carefully coach, for my mind isn't completely together right now and my body's not taking any messages. Instinct is taking over.

I notice her hesitation and heavy swallow of saliva as if she realizes how dumb she is for bringing this up here, on the pool deck, but it's too late to recover and she's still too dumb to rectify her mistake, so instead she keeps talking like the goddamn oblivious moron that she is.

"I was wondering if you would like the team to send her a card wishing her good luck on the surgery?"

My blood is boiling. Goddamn her. Why does she have to say something so fucking nice? Why does she even have to care? Doesn't she get it? I hate her. Why can't she just let me hate her in peace!

I hesitate in thought. My first reaction is definitely to say no, I don't want anyone to know, but my second reaction is that it might be nice and I shouldn't be so selfish. I try to picture myself in my mother's situation, awaiting my death sentence. I would definitely like a nice card from my son and his friends. I need to think about what's best for her. I try, but I don't always do the right thing.

I close my eyes and then open them. I stare into her naïve, well meaning, doe-like eyes staring back at me and I take a breath.

"Yeah, sure. That would be great." I want to punch myself in the fucking head. "That would be really great." I smile the fakest smile I could ever muster, but she doesn't notice a damn difference. I could bare my teeth at her and she'd react the same way. All she sees is her good deed and a smile.

"My mom is dying." I say again to Connor after a long time of sitting silently on the bench. Connor doesn't respond immediately and I don't blame him. I wouldn't know what to say either. I watch the steam form into a cloud of puffed out air as he exhales a very calm breath, almost like his lungs are struggling along with his head trying to find the right thing to say. I can tell his heart has slowed down. He's trying to feel.

"I remember" he starts off slowly, "last year when your mom had that big surgery thing and you didn't mention her again. I figured she was doing alright."

This is why I love Connor and hate him. The first words out of his mouth weren't, "I'm sorry" or "Oh my God" or "Wow, I didn't know" or "Shit, are you alright?" They are words addressing what's happened to lead to this point in time. He wants to know what happened. He's not dismissing and he is not cowering away. He's jumping right in. The problem is, in this case, I'm not sure he can tread the current.

"Yeah," I interrupt, my voice speeding along almost like it's trying to evade its own sound, "that went really well. She was doing great for awhile, you know. Things were looking better and then she had a recurrence and—," I take another deep breath, "then the recurrence was looking better and it just keeps fucking going you know? And now the doctors just told my dad that she's dying. I found out on the train ride home from Sarah's."

Sarah is my current girlfriend. She lives in New York, but goes to school in Vermont. I got to see her for a few days over fall break and it was there that my dad called me. I looked at the phone for a long moment before picking it up. My mom had been sick for a long time and never once was I the least bit worried, but looking at the phone I felt the storm coming.

His deep disappointed voice comes through, "You should speak to your mother."

Somehow I get the impression that it's my fault for having a life outside of home. "Okay," I say, a little confused, "Put her on."

"No."

"What do you mean no? Why not?"

"You should call her."

"Why, where is she?"

"She's here."

"Well, why can't you just put her on the phone then?"

"She wants you to call her."

I am so confused, but I have an idea of what's going on. "Alright, fine, I'll call her." My tone is nasty and defensive. Sometimes you have to be that way when you're hundreds of miles away from the real world.

I call her cell phone and it goes to the answering machine so I call my dad back.

"Call the house phone," he says, so I call the house phone. It also goes to voice mail. I call Dad back. He tells me to try again, so I try again. No response, I call dad back.

"What the hell is going on! Just hand her the goddamn phone!"

"Just try again." He is so calm that I want to climb through the receiver and strangle him.

"Ahhh! Fine." I hang up and redial the house phone, no answer. I call the cell phone again, no answer. House phone, voice mail, hang up, redial, voice mail, hang up, redial, voice mail, hang up. I'm confused, furious, and scared. I don't get scared. I call dad back.

"She's still not answering." I can hear him yell to her in the background.

"Honey! Honey, why aren't you picking up the phone?" I can't hear what she says, but my dad tells me that she doesn't want to speak to me right now.

"You have got to be kidding me?"

"What?"

"What the fuck is wrong with you! What's going on!"

"Don't raise your voice!" My dad yells back. His deep voice is like the roar of an awakened bear and suddenly I'm glad for his usual calm and disappointed monotone.

"YOU were the one who asked ME to fucking call! Does this not make sense
to you?"

"Well, she doesn't want to talk right now."

"Dad, give mom the phone right now or I'm going to be furious at both of you." Dad doesn't say a word, there are just a few rustling sounds in the background and then my mom's voice comes through the receiver. She sounds drained and drugged up.

"Hi."

"Hi mom." I lower my voice significantly and recline back a little. She sounds so fragile, I'm afraid my voice will break her to pieces. More fear settles in. In six whole years of her battling one type of cancer after the next I have never been afraid till now. It's the storm. "How are you?"

"I'm fine."

"Dad said you wanted to talk to me?"

"No."

"Huh?"

"No…It's fine."

"Mom, what's wrong?"

Silence. A few quiet breaths, like she's pacing herself and trying to keep her body steady.

"Nothing."

"What's wrong!" My voice gets a little louder and I'm scared because I feel her shudder for a moment and it becomes like the few seconds after a minor earthquake ends. Everyone is alright, but they're not sure.

"I don't want to worry you and ruin your vacation with Sarah. I hope you are having a fun time."

"But mo-"

"Here's your father." The weak voice says.

"Dad?"

"I'll talk to you later Drew."

"But Dad-"

"Just let it go…Call me on your way back." Click and the line goes dead.

The possibilities are endless and a million different scenarios start racing through my head. Her tumor grew or there's another one someplace else. Maybe she has three weeks left to live, maybe two weeks…one? Or maybe it's nothing. Maybe she is just tired and doesn't want to worry me too much about something trivial. Sometimes a doctor is mean to her and it gets her upset like when the doctor told her not to get breast implants because she would be dead in six months anyway. He said, "What's the point?" That's the kind of shit they say to people. But no, that doesn't work, something else is wrong.

She's like me. She doesn't want anyone to know. She wants her plane to go down with only her in it. She wants to take the burden all on her own, yet she also wants everyone to know. She knows she needs their help. I guess she doesn't know where to start. I never know where to start…

Connor nods his head up and down slowly after I tell him all of this. He's controlled and steady. It's the deepest acknowledgement one can show, no words, merely a nod. His gaze is focused on the crevices in the brick of the wall in front of us. Then the words come, as they always do. I figure I might as well start getting used to it.

"I'm sorry," he says.

"It's alright," I respond quickly, not really wanting to continue the conversation. "I've just been feeling really edgy lately and I'm afraid I'm going to snap on someone."

"Well, I'm here for you, man, and if you need to snap on anyone, you can snap on me."

"Thanks man. Thanks. That means a lot...But I don't think I'd ever snap on you."

CHAPTER THREE

I had Connor promise not to tell anyone about our conversation. I said he could tell Michelle, his girlfriend, if he wanted to, but to ask her not to say anything to anyone. He said he wasn't going to tell her. I thanked him and we went our separate ways. People always end up going their separate ways in the real fake world.

It was around mid November, only a few weeks after I discovered the news about my mom, that I started to feel it— the insanity. It starts with a slight edginess that one can't get rid of, so you mask it with a fake-hyper activeness, which therapists like to classify as "anxiety".

My mind doesn't want to think about my mother, so my body reacts instead. It's like one of those funny cartoons, like Tom and Jerry. There's a ball that Tom holds tightly in his hand and the ball shakes wildly like it has a mind of its own. The cat then tries to hold the ball steady, but then his arm starts to shake, so he tries to keep his arm steady, but then his body and legs start to shake. The ball is moving on its own. I'm shaking and there's really no way to stop it.

I become the person that everyone likes so that I'm not noticed. It is funny how that works. To not stand out, stand out completely. Conversations always go the same way: "Hey, how are you?"

"I'm good, how are you?"

"I'm good." Just don't forget to smile.

Everyone is just so fucking good with themselves. It is amazing what you can hide in this world by taking advantage of how much other people want to talk. All someone has to do is ask you how you're doing and before you know it, you won't realize that the other person has barely spoken at all, but you'll feel like you had a perfectly fine and "good" conversation. You could be living next door to a serial killer and not even know it. For the truly naïve, after your neighbor asks you how you've been doing and you've told him all the "good" stuff that is going on in your life, take note to ask him a question or two, like how he's doing and why he does his gardening at night with a sickle and an over-sized shovel? Or better yet, call the police.

You have to become social so nobody can see that there's something wrong, you have to smile so everyone thinks you are happy, and you have to have energy because you are swimming three to five hours a day followed by homework and you can't sleep. People like me should be hired by the CIA for clinical endurance trials. If you stop, you start to think, and I can't think right now.

I couldn't hide everything though and my swimming was the first to take the hit. We have two coaches on our team and the irony is that the good coach - the one who makes all the practices and knows the science behind them – is the assistant coach, and the other coach – you know, the one with the Darth Vader hair cut – is the head coach. Her job consists of walking around the pool deck telling us what we are doing wrong, talking to us if we aren't trying hard enough and pathetically attempting to comfort us if we are in pain or feeling sick. Her medical diagnosis for everything is "take some Ibuprofin".

"Hey, Kat, my arm just fell off."

"Take some ibuprofin and kick through the rest of practice."

"But Kat it really hurts."

"Take four. You can take up to 800mg safely."

There was one particular instance in which I had gone to the nurse's office: sore throat, headache, earache, and other obvious symptoms of strep throat. I had it every year for a while because my dad and I kept giving it back and forth to each other. The nurse's office concluded after a basic culture test that I had "tonselitus," which is a.k.a. their bullshit response to when they have no clue what it is you have. I knew what I had— I had strep throat. "Tonselitus." They might as well have said that I was making out with too many whores and that's why my throat hurt.

"Listen, I know I have strep. I've had it dozens of times. Can you please give me something? Anything?"

"Our culture checks for a hundred different common varieties of strep, but if it will make you feel better we will send your culture to a lab to check for some of the more rare strands."

"Yeah, please do that. I'm pretty sure I have strep."

"We'll see when the culture gets back."

"Is there anything you can give me in the mean time?"

"Just get lots of rest and drink fluids. We should have the results in by Wednesday."

"Do you think I could get a note saying exactly that for my coach? She doesn't understand anything unless it's written down."

The nurse gives me a puzzled look, obviously missing the joke, "Yes, we can do that. I'll write one up and you can collect it at the front on your way out."

"Thanks." Amazingly enough these people were more fake than me. There were stories from the girls who came in complaining that they had a headache and the nurse's forced them to take pregnancy tests.

"We think you might be pregnant," they said to one of my friends.

"But I have never even had sex! My head hurts. This is ridiculous."

"It doesn't matter. We have to make sure you are not pregnant so that we can conclude it isn't part of what's causing your symptoms."

"You're joking right?"

These girls would end up getting a bill in their mailbox for one hundred dollars. God I would have loved to tip the insurance companies off to that stupid protocol. Think about it. Only 1,000 girls across 100 schools and each time they have to go in to the nurse's office even for a headache, they are charged one hundred dollars for a pregnancy test! They would only have to go to see the nurse ten times a year and that would add up to a million dollars. And to think the insurance companies haggled with my parents for 36,000 dollars because she had to get a tumor removed. A tumor for Christ's sake!

Insurance companies investing in pregnancy tests could make enough money to cure cancer. Next they'll be asking men who come in sick for the skin cells off the heads of their penis' to find out who was the last one they'd slept with and then they'll make her get a pregnancy test. Both parties will end up with bills in the mail. You have to love a system like that.

Statistically only 500 people come down with ovarian cancer each year. At 36,000 dollars to remove a tumor, we're looking at 1.8 million dollars to remove a tumor from each one of these individuals. We allow schools to force pregnancy tests on any girl with a headache, so why not hassle the one's who are dying too, right? You can't segregate people like that.

I feel like crap as I drag my body to the swimming pool with my note in hand. I show Darth Vader the note. She takes it and looks at it, then looks at me, then back to the note.

"Oh, you only have tonselitus, that's nothing. I've had that before," she says it all chipper like and with her plastic smile. This woman makes the Stepford Wives seem human. I give her my death stare like I usually do. Apparently she's a doctor as well as a swim coach. I didn't realize being CPR certified meant you've earned a PHD.

"I'm pretty sure I have strep, Kat, it just didn't show up on their tests."

"Well, the nurse's didn't say you have strep."

I so hate this woman. Apparently she's on their level and relates to them. I'm waiting for her to ask me when the last time I had a pregnancy test was.

"They'll know for sure only once the culture comes back from the lab."

"Well, how long will that take?"

"I don't know. They said Wednesday." I suddenly realize that it will take them as much time to send out my culture as it takes most people to send out their voting ballots. No sense of urgency. They might even ask the lab to take their sweet time on getting the results back because I was a smart ass and acted like I knew when I was sick. That's their job, right? Well then, maybe they should go from door to door to normal healthy people and tell them when they are sick and when they are not. The nurse should come to my door and tell me I have lung cancer or cardiovascular disease. "But I don't smoke or eat meat."

"Doesn't matter."

We're all apparently pregnant and we don't even know it and we're all apparently dying of something or there's absolutely nothing wrong with us. We simply have whore disease, neuroses or a simple birthmark. We're all either dying or we think we're dying, but you can't *know* when you're actually sick with something and self medicate. We live in a world where you can't know something for sure. To self medicate is immoral and worse, illegal – even if it is exactly what you need. If only the world could run on common sense we would all be healthy drugged up individuals. We might even die happy on the massive amounts of morphine we inject into ourselves to finally overdose when we knew for *sure* that our time was up. You can't do that though. You can't even suspect it might be possible. Trust them, they know what's best. Just know that at any given time you could be pregnant and everything else you need to know about the real-fake world will fall into place.

"Well," she says "I can't have you out for three days simply because you suspect that you *may* actually be sick, so take some

Ibuprofin, get some rest and come back later tonight to do the workout."

By now you're probably thinking I'm this angry, bitter human being. Partially true, but I'm really only laughing. I'm laughing so fucking hard because perspective has killed my innocent image of this world. I wouldn't want to be like this woman if I was a slave in Africa. I bet she doesn't even have any pets because any animal would go psychotic and run away from her and they'd realize that she would only stand there, shocked, with that same stupid mindless expression that she has on now. She wouldn't know why, she would only accept it. Even animals have feelings. She's more like a lab rat on Perkasets.

So I imagined myself kicking her. Kicking her right in her goddamn ovaries, you know? Why there? I don't know, to make her feel *something..Anything.* Because pain is real. There is no arguing it. It is truth in pure form. And so I see myself kicking her again and again and again and again until she got kicked so many times she developed a tumor. Then I would tell her to go swim 5000 yards (200 laps) after her chemotherapy session. I would tell her that the insurance companies are right. They should be absolutely sure that you need that surgery to remove the tumor before they pay the expense for it. They should definitely make sure that your gall bladder removal 15 years ago will have no bearing on the outcome.

It's not like they're in it for the business of saving people you know? This is for money. They can't make exceptions. I would then go on and tell her she needs a note from her doctor before I let her cut swim practice. I would say to her, "No, you can't be out for that long. Three months of chemotherapy is too much. You can't have a tumor."

You think I'm being harsh? Another swimmer, my roommate Josh, came in to her office one day because he had a tumor in his ankle and needed to get surgery on it. He would be out of commission for six months and possibly need more surgery. Her response was, "You can't have a tumor in your ankle... I've never heard of that."

If only it was legal for me to kick this woman in the ovaries then maybe I could go back to my room and get some sleep. I'd rather get the workout over with though, so instead I say, "thanks" and walk straight into the locker room so that she is never given the slightest hint of anything being wrong.

Three days later, on Thursday afternoon, I received a phone call informing me that I had strep throat and needed Penicillin right away. You have to love doctors. They always manage to be just a little too late.

CHAPTER FOUR

My mother had breast cancer on and off for four years before developing ovarian cancer. She was a woman very in tuned to her own body, so when she first began feeling pain in her ovaries, she went to the "Best Gynecologist in Westchester," as rated by Westchester Magazine.

"You're fine," she said to my mother, after a basic examination. "If it's anything, it is merely a small cist. Completely normal for a woman at your age."

"No," my mom argued back authoritatively. "There's something wrong. I can *feel* it."

"Mrs. Linscott, you are overreacting. I gave you a standard overview and none of the results indicate that there's anything wrong." My mom sat still, staring hard at the so called doctor. I guess it's where I get it from, except it's not simply anger or arrogance behind her eyes, it's the electricity of life itself churning around an air that reports back to her. She knows the truth, while I can only speculate on it and what she could see from this doctor was an impatient attitude concerning the life of a human being. Apathy takes over after administering too many nonsensical pregnancy tests. "Listen, take one of my cards at the front desk and call me if anything...*significant* comes up. If not, I'll see you in a year. You can make an appointment with Melissa at the front desk."

Mom never made one year. Five months later she began bleeding and her worst nightmare came true. By June 2003, a different doctor had diagnosed her with ovarian cancer. She had a tumor the size of a walnut.

"How did you not feel this Mrs. Linscott?" her new Doctor asked. Mom could only stare back at him, blank, and lost. Inside though, she was screaming.

***

I'm sitting up in my dorm room bed, tears are coming out of my eyes and beads of sweat are on my forehead and running down the back of my neck and for a good few seconds I have no idea where I am.

They have started.

The dreams have started.

I've been running on nothing, but four hours sleep every night and the sleep I have gotten, I've been in a perpetual crisis that I can't remember. It feels like I've been awake all night, running and hiding from something I'm being chased by, but I don't know what. I don't even know why I have tears coming out of my eyes. My sheets are drenched with sweat. I check my head, but I don't have a fever. I look down from my bunk to the alarm clock which reads 5:30 AM. One more hour till practice.

I put my head back down on my pillow. I don't even care that I was screaming or what I was screaming about, all I want is to get back to sleep. When I'm awake all I want to do is to stay awake and when I'm asleep all I want to do is stay asleep.

The alarm clock goes off at 6:30 AM. I have to put my alarm at least five feet away from me or I'd hit it and go back to sleep. So I drag myself to the alarm and hit it, but I can't remember why I'm standing. Then it all comes back to me in a huge wave of memories and thoughts that my mind has tried so hard to suppress over the course of the night. "That's right," I think to myself. "I'm alive."

I stand still for two minutes, gathering my thoughts and debating whether or not to skip practice and go back to sleep. I would kill to go back to sleep. But the swim team mentality is like a family or a job; your absence will be counted and marked down. Even missing one practice means the other swim team members will gossip with each other about it and I'll have to have a conversation with Kat and personally I'd rather be bleeding out my ass than have to do that. So I give in like I always do to authority and gather up all my equipment. I head out still in my pajamas.

The walk out into the cold morning air wakes me up a little bit. The smell of the sweet gum and pine trees helps remind me that I am still alive and that there is another world outside of my own.

"This is all temporary," I remind myself. "There is more to life than this."

I get down to the pool, change into my swimsuit, and find myself standing in front of the water. Time seems to skip and jump around when you are half asleep. The big Director cuts, splices, and edits and then "Oh that's right, here I am again."

Thinking about jumping into the cold pool, I can't remember why I used to love this sport so much. It used to be freedom and now it is only a way of life.

I can feel myself breaking down and this doesn't happen to me. I don't quit, I don't give up, and I definitely don't get this pissed off at everything. Everyone on deck looks half dead and to my left, a disturbing image catches my attention.

The whiteboard is used for the "Inspirational saying" of the day. My coach, the one I'd like to kick in the ovaries, has a book called "1001 inspirational quotes". I don't think there's anything wrong with inspiration. Inspiration is good, but it should be self-desired and not shoved down your throat. Imagine a job, a job that you used to like, but has lately become extremely repetitive, difficult, and tiring. It's a full time job and you walk in at 6:45 in the morning exhausted. Now what you happen to see, before your coffee, before you even sit down, is a quote with something cheesy and inspirational that is supposed to convince you not to give up on your hard work at your job, but what's worse is the quote right next to it that reads, "smile, you're working" with a nice pretty smiley emoticon face drawn. Now change the word working to swimming and that's the mentality that coaches try to place on their athletes. Now I know why I was screaming.

I want to throw myself into a coma where I'll finally be able to get some sleep, but the day in the real fake world goes on. Class starts at 10:20 giving me an hour to eat breakfast. As I walk along the stone pathway to class, I begin to notice that there is something that has crawled inside my brain. I can feel it itching around in my head wanting to tear through the fabrics as it makes its way through brain matter, nerve endings, and memories. I picture a host virus making its way through pink fluid until it finds a nice warm place to rest for a short time. Maybe it finished swim practice, but doesn't actually rest. Instead, it works itself into a tumor. It realizes it can't cope with the world around it and so it continues trying to find a way out and it *will* find a way out. In order to accomplish this though it finds it must turn itself into something horrible, something no one else likes. The tumor then spreads more viruses to create more tumors until I have 10,000 brain matter boiling tumors ripping their way through my skull.

I want the itching to go away.

I take my seat and listen to my professor lecture. She's nice. An older woman, tall and thin with blonde hair and gray roots and somewhere in her late forties. Her voice is calm and sweet. She doesn't wear any perfumes, but if she did they would have such subtlety that anyone would be bound to like it. She always comes in wearing interesting flower design dresses. Those dresses remind me of the Botanical Gardens in New York where my mother works or I should say, used to work. She's on disability now and they are trying their best to get her fired because she is too much of a burden even after working for them for twelve years. The business world can't function around imperfections. It despises scratches on a car.

My imagination suddenly takes over. I stare at my teacher's flower design dress and the vines leading to purple tulips begin to grow and spread outside of the dress itself and fall off of it. They branch out across the ceramic tiled floor, spreading around the room, until one flower grabs my attention like a waving hand. It turns to the window and so do my eyes.

Mom would take me to the Gardens on walks, teaching me the names of different flowers and trees. I don't remember the names, they have too many words in them, but I remember what the flowers look like, I remember the walks, and I remember her and how happy she was there. We would eat at the granary while we cherished the air saturated with different aromas. Cherry blossoms were my favorite smell, pots heavily filled with rich soil was my second. I like the Earth. I like watching it unfold over time or maybe I just like watching in general.

The blinds on three large windows of the classroom are open to the outside "real world", and my focus is lost on the professor, finding comfort in the calmness of the dark breezy day. A willow tree, straight out of a gothic novel, sways ever so calmly and happily even amongst all the dreary clouds. It becomes caught in my brain as this sublime moment where everything else in the world is tuned out. It sways there like it could sway forever. I close my eyes for a second trying to sway with it, imagining myself out there standing next to it, mind blank… Swaying.

The first call of "Drew" misses my attention completely, but I jump at the second. "Drew!" my professor yells, suddenly not seeming so nice. Try taking some Valium and then going to class. This is what it feels like to have two hours of practice at seven in the morning after a night of no sleep; the world turns into one of those glass balls you find during Christmas with the fake snow inside except *you* are on the inside. Everyone else is on the outside tapping on the glass, shaking it around, trying to get your attention, but you're caught in this liquid snow floating around brainlessly. All the shaking and tapping, it feels like the whole outside world is getting ready to shatter. And sometimes, you want it to.

Her tap on the glass shoots my attention to her. She doesn't look too mad, but she has both hands on her hips akimbo style and is definitely agitated.

"Is there something more interesting outside than my lesson?" She says with a sweet smile and a finger that impatiently taps against the side of her hip.

I should tell her...

I should tell her a tree is more interesting than her lesson. I should tell her that a tree is more interesting than all the lessons she has ever given. I should tell her that I can learn more from that tree than I ever can from her. At least that tree is outside. At least that tree is alive and feels the cold. It feels the breeze touching its every branch. The leaves move in harmony with what they feel, as one organism that is alive. Even with being rooted into the ground, the very lifeblood of this planet, that tree ends up being more free than anyone else here because we are all stuck in your damn classroom learning about how to properly format a piece of paper with words on it that you couldn't even do without a fucking tree! Everything is being put into perspective.

That tree will never have to go for three years of chemotherapy. That tree will never have to sit on the toilet bowl for two hours trying to squeeze out a shit the size of a marble. That tree will never wail in horrifying agony and moan from the deepest exhaustion that leaves you wanting to kill yourself. That tree will not cry itself to sleep at night. That tree will never have to seek a psychologist, a psychiatrist, self-help groups, meditation therapy, acupuncture, and undergo so many surgeries that the doctors can't even find your veins anymore. Nobody is putting a hole in the tree's chest so that a doctor can inject more medications into it. That tree doesn't have to have its breasts, ovaries and rectum removed, and then have a doctor poke around its insides for twelve hours looking for tumors.

Is this getting across to you yet, Mrs. Professor? Doctor Bullshit? Whatever you want to consider yourself, because whatever it is you don't deserve it! I'm fucking telling you, wake the fuck up because your names are chuck full of lies. It's all lies! Yes, that tree is more fucking interesting than your goddamn, piss ass excuse for a lesson!

But she's nice and I wouldn't say any of that to her...

"No," I say. "I'm sorry, I guess I'm just out of it today."

"Okay then," she says. "Let's get back to the lesson."

CHAPTER FIVE

I taste the sweet burn of alcohol pouring down into my soul. The trident of the devil himself is piercing my heart and twisting with all his might, laughing maliciously. He is trying to destroy me. I want him to destroy me and at least it makes my head feel better.

I'm on my seventh drink of the night, but I'm pretty sober because I'm watching after two of my girl friends who are completely obliterated or at least pretending they are so that boys will hit on them. Girls, and by girls I mean the real fake world girls, never know how much trouble they can get in when they're drunk until they are actually in trouble. The worst thing about these types of girls is that some of them will ditch their best friend for a guy in a heartbeat without thinking twice. Guys do this all the time, but guys don't usually worry about their friends being raped, they'll just wake up in the morning and say, "oops, where'd she come from?" These girls I'm looking after are best friends, but I've seen each of them ditch the other for a boy. They're not real friends, more like acquaintances with common bonds who have been thrown together in a similar location and happened to connect right away— they just call themselves best friends. Language is strange like that, it never gets to the heart of anything so you call it the wrong name forever and forever and forever. Some say these wrong words repetitiously, and some do it ignorantly, and some do it naturally, and some do it fakely to be machiavellian, and some do it fakely because they don't know what else to do, and some do it fakely just to be heard and noticed. The sad irony is that at the end of the day nobody really knows anyone else, and all this fakery is at the expense of not wanting to be alone. We're changing who we are to go forwards and wind up exactly where we started, but worse because we no longer know ourselves. We're all "good". Not many people care enough to wonder what is beyond the word "good" and a smile and how your day was and you really will accept almost any answer that is given as long as it's within the realms of what you're used to. This is at the heart of why we feel inclined to drink ourselves into comas; it's the only way we can finally start knowing one another.

We're at the swimmer's house, a.k.a. "The Blue House". Not because water is blue or anything, but because the actual house itself is blue. It works as a double entendre. There are more drinks and I've lost count in the darkness with the beat of the music blasting its way through everything, trying to break it all. I can feel it going right to my brain killing me and it feels good not to care. A generation of kids who are handed the world on a silver platter and we don't want to care. Moms and Dads struggling hard to keep their families on their feet, working day in and day out, maybe even staying with someone they don't love or a job they hate for the sake of their children. Meanwhile the kids are sweeping out the carpet from under them showing them why they shouldn't even bother. It's like we're all investments and we don't feel much like being treated as stocks anymore. Then again we like the monetary benefits.

I've been doing this to mom and dad for a long time now, trying to kill myself without actually doing it. I'm not suicidal. I simply want to forget or not care for a few hours of the day, but how does that boil down? For those few hours I don't want to be alive. I don't want to be dead permanently, just for a brief period of time, but how is that any different? If I really knew people, I wouldn't have to do this. If I could talk to people and I mean really talk to them, I wouldn't have to do this. If I could make love to women who opened up to me and weren't afraid of their image or what their friends would say or the fact that I have green eyes and not blue, I wouldn't have to do this. If I knew that while I was in this safe world, everyone else was too, maybe I wouldn't have to do this. If I knew that there weren't people dying alone or hungry on some street somewhere, or that some kid wasn't stabbing another kid merely because he could, maybe then I wouldn't have to do this. If there weren't kids my age fighting in a war, getting their legs blown off, having their girlfriends or wives cheat on them while they're away while I learn how to format a piece of paper in a classroom, maybe then I wouldn't have to do this. If my mom wasn't dying and losing her mind, her hair, and her memories and taking it all out on my father and I, then maybe I wouldn't have to do this. In the real fake world you don't need to care because it's not about them— the parents. We didn't choose this life, it chose us. They gave it to us, so who says we can't throw it all away? Are we responsible for our actions or are we not? Why do you want us so safe when there is so little here to save?

In my death state, I'm closer to her now then when I'm ten feet away simply being one step in either direction: life one step this way and death one step that way. Here, I am toying with the in between and that makes me free. When there are no rules, imagination is at its peek, and the veil covering the real fake world lifts itself up to what truly exists.

Even after all their drunkenness, most kids will never go the rest of the way, and even if they do, it's always "an accident". Johnny "accidentally" drank too much and his heart stopped beating. Few actually stop and make the conscious effort to go the rest of the way. "How did poor Johnny die?"

"Alcohol Poisoning."

No, it's suicide! It's all slow, yet purposeful suicide! Wake up! Sociologist's statistical data would go off the charts if they only changed the terms.

I'm so close…

I can see her when I close my eyes and when I dream. My forever drunken dream of how she used to be, how our family used to be, before she lost all her hair, before she was tired all the time. Then I can smile and float away.

But I'm not like that. "Noel…Jen…let's get out of here."
They are both so drunk that they are falling over each other. It's a
cold crisp night and the stars are shining in the Maryland sky. Most
people exit a house and look around, but I look up. We're here, in
this intoxicated state because everything is so overwhelming and we
can't take it sometimes. I can't breathe in the real fake world. I'm not
rooted to the ground like the trees. We're all floating leaves from a
forgotten tree that we lost somewhere along the way.

When I feel like this, though, I remember to breathe it all in
and let the world hit me with everything it has because I'm not afraid
here. There is something real in this moment. I can look up at the
stars and breathe it in, absorbing it all into my veins. The ultimate
heroin is to accept everything for what it is, close your eyes, and
breathe. That moment is perfect and I hold it in as long as I can.

My eyes open. Noel stumbles up the hill and then stops
suddenly. "What time is it?"
I look at my watch, "About 12:15."
"What! Why are we heading back, it's so early."
The real world tells me to head back, "Well, I'm heading back."
"Okay, you go back, but Jen and I are heading back to the party.
Come on Jen." She calls her friend like she's a dog and she pretty
much is to her. Her voice is all high pitched and nasally like she's
twelve years old again. I can't leave them by themselves and they
don't understand why I care. If I grabbed them right now and forced

them to go back to their rooms to save them, they'd slap me or kick me. They would say "Let go of me, I can take care of myself." Then they would trip over their own feet, fall to the ground, and scrape themselves. They would get up with blood on their arms, unable to look up, and they would skip and laugh back to the party. It's no wonder that rape happens so frequently. Noel is only looking for a hook up and she'll sacrifice her best friend to do it. Remember this, in the real fake world if I'm only 65% correct, then I still pass. Try explaining this to a police officer or a judge and see how they respond.

They start heading back down the hill. I gaze down at them as they stumble and giggle, drawing complete attention to themselves. I notice several people standing outside the house and I think to myself how stupid that is. I take one last look up the hill before turning back to go after them.

We're playing a drinking game, but before I'm even aware of it, the entire party starts to move in one fluid motion like a strong gust of wind waved over everyone. A whisper goes through the crowds. Cops! People start scattering in directions that I never knew existed. One of my friends who owns the house had pulled me aside a few months before. He told me that he had spoken to the police about the parties they had. He said that the police told him that if they came around, not to run, and that they would only ask us to break up the party and nothing more. My friend thought this was extremely fair and so he asked me specifically not to run if anything were to happen. The police came only one time before: they asked us to break the party up, thanked us for cooperating, and went on their way. We didn't continue the party.

On this specific instance those who ran, escaped, and those who cooperated were made to sit down and be breathalized. Noel and Jen ran.

I walk outside the front door of the blue house and one cop in a bright yellow shirt acts as if we all committed murder and he shoves his flashlight hard into our faces and speaks like the devil would to God— trying to establish his authority— while God sits back passively wondering what the hell this odd creature is so mad about. I wonder what the drinking age was back when Jesus was around.

I know this cop. I know him very well. He wears a cross. He might even have a cross tattoo. He is the type back in high school who drove 130mph with his friends in the car, drinking a beer and laughing about it. In grade school he was the one who bullied kids and set ladybugs on fire with a magnifying glass. He kicked stray dogs for fun and shot bb guns at squirrels. This is the kid who would have raped my two friends if I hadn't gone back for them.

I know his kind and here he is sticking his cock lantern in my face, thinking that all it takes to be *right* and to be *real* is to have a badge. I pretend to know him because he pretends to know me. And all I wanted to do was have a night of suicidal fun. In America, I guess you have to be 21 to want to kill yourself.

CHAPTER SIX

I tell her, "I always have this problem that I never know where to start."

"Well, what would you like to talk about?" she asks.

"Videotapes."

That night of drinking we were never actually arrested; we were mandated to take alcohol classes administered by the state and the school required we attend a class of our own.

"I won't go."

An Asian woman with a white button down shirt and a tie looks up from the file that's curled up in her lap and she stares at me through her glasses. The three-year-olds had it right all along, we should have stuck to saying no to everything.

"What do you mean you won't go?"

"I won't go."

"Well, you have to go."

"Why?"

"Listen, it's only an hour. The school requires that you take the class—"

"How about an alternative?"

She sits back in her seat and folds her hands on her lap. "What did you have in mind?"

I breathe. "Alcohol classes aren't really going to do anything for me, neither is it going to do anything for anyone else, but that's another matter. I simply have problems that won't be solved with alcohol classes."

"So what is it that you would like to do? I have to have you do something?"

I hate her for making me say it, but I know I have to. I breathe. "I'd like to see one of the therapists on campus. I'll see her for whatever amount of time you'd like, just please don't make me go to another alcohol class."

"Hmm..." she says, thinking it over, "You are sure about this?"

"Yes, very sure." I had been thinking about it for a while, but didn't know how to approach it.

"Okay, I'll see what I can do." She takes out a pen and a binder from under her desk. Inside are a few loose rectangular pieces of paper, which she starts filling out. "You will be required to see her for three sessions and beyond that, it's your choice. I'll make you an appointment so that you don't have to."

I like this woman. "Thank you."

"Videotapes." I say to Jessica, my new therapist. I had tried therapy before her and I never got passed the first day, but something about Jessica was different: she has bright blue eyes that are glassy with life, but reflect only emptiness. She opens them wide and keeps them like that. I like this characteristic of hers because it means I can't read her. It's as if she already knows my kind, the one who will turn conversation away from ones self, pushing everything away. I call it manipulation, but I'm really only manipulating myself. This is what she wants me to learn. I can learn a lot about myself from Jessica.

She has dirty blonde hair, which falls straight down behind her back and over her thin slender shoulders, which I suddenly have the urge to kiss. She's smart, though. She's wearing an aqua colored sweater, which covers her entire torso and rises up a half inch on her neck so I can't even imagine myself kissing her in that way for very long. She stops my imagination. My escape. She's already put me into place and she's barely said a word; sitting there still as an icy goddess, staring at me. It's like she opened my file and it read, "Is highly sexual, a manipulative asshole, an alcoholic, an anarchist of society, suffers from emotional turmoil, and wouldn't hurt anyone because of his profound empathy." Her, sitting there, staring at me, she's like a beautiful blow up doll with the dress code of a nun, not a person and she knows that's what I need in order to be able to focus on talking. My first day and I already understand the sexual tension that goes along with therapy, but that's all thrown out the window, especially after my gaze finishes scanning her body and lands on her left hand which has a silver ring on the index finger.

"Videotapes," I tell Jessica. "My mother was going through the videotapes and DVD's in my room- shuffling through them, moving them with such jittery haste to make anyone frightened- like she was possessed or on coke, or speed. She hustled around in a frantic panic like her very life was in danger." It was in danger. Anxiety reaches the pinnacle point in my throat before I can even get words out of my mouth.

"What are you doing?" My words, directed towards my mother, come out surprisingly calm for finding my room being rummaged through. She doesn't respond. She won't even do me the favor of responding to my calm words. Her old words come back to me:

"You spoiled brat, you're a spoiled brat! You don't give a shit about anyone!"   These words echo in my head as I think, "This is my room. MY room. Does that make me spoiled? YES!" Possession makes me spoiled and gifts are gifts. You don't take them back.

"What are you fucking doing!" I scream at her. She could have asked. Any decent human being talks, but she just acts on instinct. Her whole being is based on instinct— a true specimen mix of both the real and fake worlds.

"I'm taking my movies back," she says quickly and without tone.

"What movies?" I walk over to her to get a better look at the movies. "Those are my movies. I just bought them."

"Oh Yeah," she screams and I find myself on the front lines of a battlefield filled with landmines that she places strategically after my every word. "How about this one!" She shoves *American Beauty* within two inches of my face and I can't help but think of the irony. "And this one!" She shoves *5th Element* in my face. "And this…These are my movies and you took them all from upstairs and dumped them down here."

I back up, disgusted by the spit that's flying out of her mouth like venom and the objects that have lividly been thrown in my face. It's uncalled for animosity, but you have to understand that she can't remember. She can't reflect. She's looking death in the face and all she can think about are the videotapes she'll never be able to watch again. Her memory is failing and with it are her misplaced videotapes. A slideshow of countless emotions mixed with time spent with my father and I, all dumped. That's what her life comes down to. I feel my life coming down to it too.

Sadly, I know all of this, but it doesn't matter because I won't take her for a dying woman. She doesn't understand that we're fighting the same battle merely on opposite sides.

"First of all…" Picture ocean water as it tries to put out a volcano – my voice tries to maintain a level of calmness. I am a white feather in a light breeze, "I brought those DVD's and videotapes down here because yours were piling up and falling out of the cupboard every time I tried to open it, so I decided to make some room down here to put them nice and neatly with the names face up in a way that you can see each and every one of them instead of having to DUMP fifty of them out in order to find the one you're looking for. Secondly, you don't watch these movies any—."

I know what's coming before the words have even left my mouth. You could write an entire book and people will focus on only one thing you've said. Everything else is just a dumped videotape.

"I do watch these movies, and they are MY movies you arrogant little prick!" Reflect back to MY room…yeah this is where I get it from. "And even if I didn't, I want to be able to find them when I want to because they are MY FUCKING MOVIES!" She says this last part with a wild shake of her head like how a great male lion shakes its mane except I think I'd rather face the lion. It's not smart to argue with a lion, but then again my SAT scores aren't that great. I hear my dad's panicked voice from way upstairs, "What's going on?" Followed by the speedy race of footsteps.

"No you don't watch them! You haven't watched an old movie in years, you only rent new ones. I'm the only one who watches these and if you, *by chance*, are to watch an older movie, which happens once every three years or so, then you will be able to walk the ONE FLIGHT of stairs down to MY room, find it because you'll actually be able to see where it is and then you can watch it all you fucking want."

Like a banshee born from hell, "WILLLIAAAM!!!!" Adding in a third person is her way of winning the defensive. She's trying to exhaust me because she knows she can. I hate saying everything over again, but luckily I had told him all of this the day before while I was organizing.

His run down the final flight of steps sends sheer panic through my veins as my heart escalates to the beat. He steps in and observes the completely non-life threatening situation, but an ere of skepticism remains.

"What?…What the hell's the matter with you!" he says, directing his attention at my mother.

"Your son won't give me back my movies. He's moved everything down here and is hording it and says they are all his…see this! This is ours, isn't it? Tell him William."

The movie she holds up, I have no idea whether it's hers or mine. I roll my eyes at her manipulativeness. My father looks towards me as if he's waiting for me to say something. He's defending her already: his wide eyes, his weight pressed in my direction, even his hair has straightened out and is pointing at me. The energy is so thick with anger it could run a turbine engine and I'm about to be put right through the center of it. I'm going to lose, but losing doesn't matter, fighting matters. I have to fight the real world and the fake world until I find my place, until my life finds harmony. Nobody challenges my struggle for peace more than her. For everyone else I let it slide: for Conner, for Kat, for the hypocrite police officer, for the girls who call themselves best friends, for my professor, for this whole fucking world I let it slide, but for her I let her know it all. This is what I'm getting at with Jessica. This is what videotapes are about. For my mom, I could blame her for everything. I'm trying my best to organize the world she brought me into, make sense of it, put the videotapes in an organized and manageable manner and there she goes again and blows it all to hell. I just can't win. My dad's famous words come through my head, "Son, you can be right, but still be wrong." Well, fuck it, you can't be either when you're dead, so I might as well get my time in and so should she. I can't let her think she's going to die. She needs to know that she has to live to fight and fight to live.

"What are you a fucking idiot! Are you that fucking stupid that you don't listen to one word I say. I'm trying to tell you that-." I have friends who tell me they have never cursed at their parents and some say their parents rarely fight. I don't know that world.

"--Don't talk to your mother like that!"

"Dad just listen to me, okay? I told you all of this yesterday. I'm only trying to help—."

"All I see is that you're upsetting your mother. You know the fragile state she's in. Just put the movies back."

"Dad, *some* of these movies I recently bought from the store. I'm telling you, I went to Best Buy yesterday. I might even still have the receipt around somewhere." I look around frantically for a bag, a small slip of paper...anything. I wished to God I had kept the receipt if only to rub it back in her face at the approximate distance of two inches. I would then watch as the ink makes its way off the paper to her face, into her mouth and is somehow digested by both her stomach and brain, but the truth is that the truth doesn't matter. There is no truth here.

"I wanted a few to take back to college with me."

"No!" The banshee screams… "No! No! No! Noooooo! These are mine! You stole them from me! You stole them!"

"Will you calm down?" Dad asks.

Mom turns to Dad wielding a look that could bring the rock of Gibraltar crashing into the sea.

"Are you taking his side!? I want to watch these movies…look, well, not this one" she puts down *Fight Club* and I smile at the continuing irony of why I bought these movies in the first place. "But this one, and this one; these are mine, aren't they William! Tell him!"

"Drew, please put the movies back."

"No, I'm not putting them back! What the fuck is wrong with you people. I'm not taking them, I'm not stealing them, they are going to be down here where you can walk down the stairs any time you want and get them. Or else maybe you should buy another cupboard so the DVD's can be properly organized."

"You just said you were taking them to college."

I let out a heavy sigh, "Those movies, yes, because I just bought those, with my own money, but the rest are here. If you're missing movies I'll even go out back to Best Buy and get them for you. It's no problem."

"I want all my movies back in their cases and in the cabinet in five minutes and if I'm missing a movie that I know I have, God help you because you will be in so much trouble you can't even fathom it."

"Are you kidding me? I said I'd go out and buy them for you. Are you insane?"

Mom doesn't even bother listening anymore as she turns her back and storms out of the room. I turn to dad.

"What the hell is wrong with her?"

"Don't raise your voice"

"I wasn't raising my—."

"You're horrible to her. Can't you just put the movies back like she asks?"

"But—."

"She's sick Drew, don't you understand that?"

"You're a fucking hypocrite, you know that! Imagine her going through your drawers in your room and moving around all of your stuff claiming back everything she said was hers. She takes over. Look at the kitchen table! We don't even have a place to sit down and eat because she's piled papers all over it. She even took over the desk that both of you were supposed to use. You don't stand up for yourself."

"Stop it."

"Look, I'll even buy you something where you'll be able to see all the movies, and I'll bring everything upstairs. The two of you are just fucking morons."

"Stop it." He starts moving towards me with rage in his eyes.

"You're pathetic! What is wrong with you! You can't even see how stupid it is to have them falling out like that."

"Drew, shut up."

"You—."

"Drew, shut the hell up."

"No, no! I won't shut—"

"Drew!" I see him raise his hand to me, but the blow never comes as I cover my hands in front of my face being the coward that I am.

"Movies, videotapes, DVD's," I tell Jessica. "This is why I'm here. The doctors say my mother is dying and she wants her videotapes back where she put them."

CHAPTER SEVEN

It was Kindergarten at age six when I first encountered death. I had heard about my Grandfather on my father's side dying when I was five, but he lived in Florida, and I didn't watch him die.

I open my eyes to a large glass container. A bright light shines onto yellow straw with white oval shells resting on them. It's one of those moments where you wake up as if you're seeing the world for the first time. They always seem to make a memory.

I watch Richard and Joseph tap on the glass causing the eggs to shift around in their niche. They giggle and point at the eggs they can move around the most with their continuous rapping. Richard turns to face Joseph, "See that big one, that's my egg".

Joseph turns to Richard, "Oh yeah, well that bigger one over there is my egg."

"Uh, uh. Mine's the biggest."

The teacher steps in, "Joseph, Richard, get away from the incubator, now!" Richard and Joseph giggle and take their seats. "I don't want to catch you two by it again. You don't want to harm your eggs do you?" They laugh. "Class, no one is allowed near the incubators anymore, that means you too, Drew."

I stop staring at the incubator to look at her. She's petite with the presence of a giant due to her sweet voice and yet stern disposition. She's the type who always has to move her hands when she speaks and has a continuous Contra Pasto pose like she's modeling for twenty six-year-olds who haven't even discovered their own genitals yet might as well be judging her style. She's dressed like a catholic sunflower: almost no skin showing, but with bright colorful yellows. I give her a look of disappointment before going back to my seat. Richard turns to Joseph, "Now he can't stare at 'em all the time. What a dork." They laugh. Staying still in my seat, I look down to the floor and think about how I don't have an egg. I didn't claim one as my own. I didn't fight or argue. I figured I would take the egg my teacher gave me and that would be the egg that was meant for me. My gaze strays back to the two kids laughing. I didn't understand their laughter, but I knew that we were all anxious for our eggs to hatch.

Weeks pass, which feels like years before I wake up again. We're all just waking moments in time waiting for the next waking moment. Everything else is a dumped videotape.

I'm holding an oval egg in my cupped out hands. I see all its nicks and imperfections and little black dots that cover the outside. The egg shape is unique and perfectly balances its pressure points that such fragile shells rarely break. If you could balance a heavy book on top of it, it would support its weight. Nature is the source of everything. The shape of light bulbs came from the shape of the egg. Even its white shade gives it a holy presence.

The teacher came over and placed it there asking me to be careful. Sitting there, cupped in my hands, it becomes my own little egg world and I can finally just stare.

I look around to see the other kids holding their eggs. The teacher yells at them not to shake them or tear the shells off. Everyone waits and at no other time would you get so many six-year-olds this quiet. Amidst the cone of silence, I think I hear the small cracking noise even before the high girlish voice of one of my peers.

"It's opening. Mine's opening!" Like falling dominoes, one kid after the other begins shouting the same thing. My anticipation escalates and I go back and stare at my egg, waiting for the slightest crack. Watching. I wait and wait and wait, but nothing.

I turn again to see small heads the size of fingernails popped out of the top of shells. The kids peel off bits and pieces trying to help and the teacher yells at them again, "you have to let them do it on their own."

A small crunching noise catches my attention and my head whips around almost fast enough to dislodge it from my neck. I see a small crack in the shell. Another light crunch and another small crack appears slightly lower down from the first. Then there's another and another. My eyes open wider with each new crack. I start yelling like all the other kids, "It's opening. Mine's opening!" I have the urge to rip the shell pieces off and tear him free, but I remember the teacher's words and resist.

Then it happens. The miracle of life. I watch as the head of the goo covered duck pops his head out just a little. The hard pressured shell working against its own purpose of existence, forcing the duck to break the perfect protection of the world around itself just to live. The head tries again and the shell lifts off a little more. A third time, and I watch as the shell falls weakly over and onto the ground. The head sticks out further and further. My heart jumps as I wait for him to spring to life. There's a tiny cry that forms from his still goo sealed mouth and then his head falls over to the side. Then nothing.

A long silence ensues where the sounds of the other children are drowned out of existence. Background colors blend into a mix of all reds and oranges, shades dissolve and I wait and wait some more, but there's only silence, an egg, a static head, and a lone boy who only watched it all.

"Miss Cassey!" I scream and the teacher runs over.

"What's the matter, sweety?"

"He stopped moving." I look down at my duck whose head is cocked to its side, still, his eyes shut, swallowed up in goo or is it blood? Miss Cassey removes a couple of shells to get a better look.

She stares for a long minute before shaking her head, "I'm sorry, honey."

"What happened?"

"I…" she hesitates and looks in the direction that she wishes to run off to. "I don't know." She turns and walks off with my egg in her hand.

There were other children whose eggs didn't hatch at all. I watched the teacher pull them over to the side, one by one, giving them her adult lie, but she wouldn't lie to me. Why wouldn't she lie to me? She wouldn't even explain what happened, though I don't think anyone could. The kids whose eggs didn't hatch were given extra ducks to take care of. I didn't ask for another and I wasn't given one. I watched as Richard and Phil laughed and played with their ducks, which grew day by day. They swam in a small plastic pool along with the rest of the ducks outside our classroom. The two pitched wars, with their ducks always ending in superiority and if they didn't, they would threaten to beat the kid up who challenged them. If you can't win inside the game, take it outside the game. Phil and Richard the conquerors. I couldn't help but think that maybe they conquered my duck too, all their tapping and shaking of the glass. I wondered, in such a large world, where the glass is shaken so often, whether my duck was a Richard or a Drew. Either way, I allowed the glass to shake, while they won at all costs. I couldn't tell if one way was better than the other; whether one was right and one was wrong.

Phil later died of sickle cell Anemia and Richard drove himself into a tree speeding too fast down a hill. We all have to lose sometime.

CHAPTER EIGHT

I was seven when my father found two baby mice left alone in our basement closet. I think he was a little annoyed that I had snuck up behind him, wondering what he was looking at. There on a silver air duct lay two baby mice, white as snow with pink little feet, sniffing aimlessly into the air.

Dad said they were White Footed mice, because the underbellies and feet are white, although not when they are very young. These two baby mice were shaking, squiggling around with unopened eyes, trying to find their way with their up pointed noses. One stopped, curled into a ball, and began shivering from the cold steel completely helpless. I look up at dad.

"What are you going to do with 'em?" Dad knew it was over then and I could see in his eyes that he wasn't happy, but I could also see the end of his lip curl into a smile at seeing me care so much for such a small animal. He takes a giant dad like breath.

"I caught the mother in the trap this morning and I'm pretty sure I got the father yesterday. I had a suspicion there was a family and went searching for them. Come, let's go see if we can get some supplies." My heart flutters and a huge grin comes across my face.

The first thing we do is cut up an old towel, using them as blankets to wrap the baby mice in. Then we take an old glass tank and make a cage for them, placing another towel down on the bottom. I watch dad work like I was in my own little cage, seeing as he tried so hard to save the same lives that he had just put in danger.

We take a small plastic cup, punch a hole in it, and then attach it to a metal nipple. Dad fills this with milk and then clamps it to the ceiling of the cage. "You see," he says, "We need to recreate the mother environment for them and see if they respond to it. If they do, they may have a chance. Chances are they won't though, so don't get your hopes up." We place the mice in the cage. They take a long time to start moving after cowering from just being lifted off the ground and taken for a ride. One of them goes for the nipple, while the other sinks back down and curls into a ball after lifting up his nose and not finding anything. It's the same one as before.

"He won't last the night," Dad says solemnly.

I watch as the healthy one sniffs his way over to the nipple, his undeveloped eyes closed and unaware. After a small nourishment, the baby mouse sniffs his way over to his little brother and curls up into him, bunching themselves up in the warm towel. I fall asleep watching.

Dreams are like memories: some you can see so clearly, some are forgotten at the blow of the wind, and both are so fragile that they may never have happened at all. I dream that my dad's arms wrap around me and he carries me off to my bedroom. I dream about taking care of a small mouse and watching him grow bigger and stronger. I dream about one day setting him free so that he may start his own mouse family far away from here and he'll know to stay away from houses so that he'll be able to watch his kid grow big and strong till he can set him free too. Then I dream about waking up and so I do.

There's a small ray of sunlight coming through the bottom of the window. Once I gain full consciousness, my body bolts upright and I throw the sheets off me, almost tripping over them as I get out of bed. I run down the stairs flinging open every door that gets in the way. Heart racing, I get to the very bottom and turn the corner to face the cage, but I can see from far away that there is a white piece of paper attached to the outside of it. Cautiously I approach, not wanting to see what it is that I know I will see. The cage is empty.

The note is from dad:

Drew,

The mice died in the middle

of the night. I didn't want to

wake you. I threw them away

in the trash.

Sorry,

Dad

I read the note over and over again. A hundred thoughts run through my head, the most powerful being, "how could he have just thrown them away? Like garbage." I didn't believe it and I thought maybe they had escaped. I ran around the house looking for the mice, retracing our steps from yesterday thinking that maybe they tried to go back home. I thought maybe they didn't die and he had gone through his original plan because I knew he didn't want to keep them, but I didn't think he would do that. Dad wasn't like that. I come back to the cage and look closer at it, thinking that maybe they are hiding in it somewhere. I pick up the towel and feel around, imagining one of them sticking his head out from under it, looking up at me with healthy eyes.

The cage was empty though and it was like everything we had done was erased. All that we tried added up to nothing and for the first time in my life, I cried over death. Cried with my head buried under the pillow of my couch. For minutes, I cried over a couple of mice. I hated crying. I hated the feelings that came with it. I kept thinking over and over again about their small delicate bodies lying in the bottom of the trashcan and I couldn't understand it.

Sadness turned to confusion. The new understanding became: all lives are not equal and you can give any life meaning. The adult mice could have been trash, but not the baby mice. Even a cockroach can become a lonely child's best friend, but all the Richards and Josephs could always just step on them and laugh.

Thinking about it over and over again, turning it up and down and around in my brain, like dreaming with a high fever, I finally reasoned it out. I forced the tears to stop. I decided to take control of my emotions and shake the glass, becoming another Richard, another Joseph, becoming everything you've ever hated just to make the tears stop, and they did stop, and I knew that I would have to never truly love anything ever again.

CHAPTER NINE

When I was twelve, my Grandmother died in the back seat of a cab. The cab driver happened to notice and was able to drive her right to the hospital. They were luckily passing one at the exact moment it occurred.

I hear all this over the phone.

"So wait, Grandma's dead?"

"No." Dad says and says nothing more.

"I thought you just said she died?"

"She did, but they brought her back at the hospital. She's suffered some brain damage and she needs to have major heart surgery."

"Oh my God. Dad, what? Why didn't you say that before?"

"Say what before?"

"Before, you know, before you said she had died."

"Because that's how it happened."

"Oh, jeeze. Okay, dad, whatever. So do they know what happened? Is she alright now?"

You find yourself never knowing the right thing to say because in your mind the person you're talking about is always fine and is always the way you remembered them to be. People can't all of a sudden die. We can't end up being at the bottom of a trashcan in the morning.

"Just come home, Drew. We're all going to go see her."

"Okay."

I hang up the phone, dazed. My grandmother was dead and now she's not. They tell me later all about how one of the valves to her heart is no longer working properly and how she needs a pacemaker. They skip the part about her relapse of cancer.

My grandmother used to have humongous boobs. She could turn in cramped areas and knock people over. You think big and if you're a man you're thinking double D's, but these were more like taking two sperm whales and attaching them to the chest of a seal. If she ever caught a cute guy staring, she'd turn to him, "It's okay sweety, you can grab 'em," and she'd give them a shake. She would pinch waiters' asses as they walked by causing them to nearly topple a full tray of food. This is when she was old. When she was young she would flash construction workers out building windows and juggle them at teachers while they drew on the chalkboard. My grandfather was the only one not impressed, so she married him.

My mother was constantly embarrassed at these frequent flirtations while her father stood idly by reading the newspaper.

"How can you let her do that?"

He'd peer up from his paper, and look at the goings on, "Do what?"

"Do...*that*?"

He'd shrug his shoulders and go back to the paper. Grandma flirted and strutted her stuff, but that's as far as she ever went with it.

When she lost her first breast, it was like half her soul went with it. When she lost the second, she didn't talk as much. She mostly looked down to the side in a daze, like she had forgotten something and couldn't remember what it was. She had beaten cancer at age forty, with both her battleships intact. It was only at age eighty-one, after the cab incident, that it came back to haunt her.

I wake up in a hospital.

We're walking into her room and a distinct aroma of dry cool air mixed with idle skin and a hint of urine enters my nostrils. There are wires hooked into Grandma's right arm by the elbow; her leathery old skin appears as if it was stretched out and then scrunched back together like plastic wrap. There's a strip of medical tape there. Her gray hair is flying out in different directions making her look like an old picture of Einstein. Propped up in a blue hospital gown, she gives us all a big smile.

"They've banned me to the bed because I kept mooning the doctors," she laughs, but midway through, she starts coughing.

"Here Grandma," I approach her, a little scared and cautious, "I brought you this." It's a little brown and tan plush puppy with a happy face and a tiny black nose. I purchased it in the gift shop on the way up. I hand it to her.

"Awwww, thank you sweety," and she smiles at me with a tear in her eye.

Mom speaks, "How are you feeling, ma?"

"Oh, honey. It's right here." She points to her chest. "It's like there's a rock," she sits up a little and shuts her eyes tight in pain, "eh, just sitting there. I look good though, don't I?"

Mom smiles, "Yeah, ma, you look terrific."

"Not bad for someone who died, right?" Grandma turns to me, "I died, you know?" She smiles proudly at me, like she climbed Mount Everest. "If it wasn't for the nice young man in the cab, I wouldn't be here."

We later found out that he was a criminal on the run and being a cab driver was his cover. He may have been a hero or he may have been only covering his ass. A dead person in the back of his car probably wouldn't have helped his cover.

"I don't know where he ran off to in such a hurry."

"Probably had to finish his shift," Dad chimes in.

"I'll see if I can get the paper to do an issue on him," says Mom.

"Oh yes, that would be wonderful. Such a nice young man, you know, I wouldn't be here if it wasn't for him."

"Ma, you're repeating yourself again."

"No, I'm not. I want to make sure you know it is all."

I see grandpa's head turn to the door before the sound even comes and I instinctually look with him. Suddenly there's a knock and a doctor enters.

"Am I interrupting?" A man in the typical holy-ware coat with thick black hair steps through the door, a smile on his face. He has thick circular glasses on.

"Good afternoon Mrs. Beaumont. I hear your butt is famous around here already."

Grandma chuckles. "Wait till you get to see the rest of me," she says as she shimmies her body.

The doctor laughs awkwardly. "Ha-ha…well then, I'm glad to see you're in good spirits. My name is doctor Phillis and I'm the one who worked on you when you came in."

"What happened?" Mom blurts out as she takes a seat and covers her mouth with her left hand. It's the shock.

The doctor looks down at his chart as if he's saved a thousand lives in between the time he saved my Grandmother's and he's having a hard time remembering. The truth is he really doesn't want to make eye contact, even through the glasses. You have to picture yourself going through four years of college forcing yourself to deal with the basic facts. The memorization bullshit. Like having to know the recipes to thousands of different foods, completely cutting you off from creativity. Then you enter four more years of med school and that's if you were even lucky enough to pass over a post-bach program and it's here that your chef career takes you to working with more of the hands on stuff. You start from scratch with all dead animal's organs sliced up and lying on a table. See this, you can make salami out of this. See that...that's a hotdog. Flesh, skin and blood sprawled out for you to see and dissect followed by more memorization.

You can't merely know what the liver is, what it looks like, what it *feels* like. you have to know its given name. Add on, additional memorization. Then you have two more years of internships where you pay the farm to allow you to work on the live animals, the one's that are still breathing. Now you can be creative because you're paying for the liability, but you've probably forgotten what being creative means. After eight to ten years of memorization and hacking away at all the different organs, you are finally a full-fledged cook who can take a live cattle and make Filet Mignon. The only problem is after all the hacking away over the years you no longer like food and after all of those years of learning you walk across the street, all proud of yourself, and you end up getting hit by a car. Your brains splatter on the pavement and all that memorization turns into ground beef again. It keeps getting run over by more and more cars until they disappear like they never were.

You have to do something, everyday, with the knowledge you're given, not use it after eight years of life have gone by. This is your life, Doctor Phillis who wears glasses. Doctors forget that they once upon a time cared so much for people that they would stop at nothing to help them, but after they've gone through the system and we're only another cattle in the herd passing through their doors. Through the glasses, we are all Filet Mignon and we don't even know it.

The doctor takes a look at all of us, especially me. He can lay his eyes on me only for a split second through those spectacles before he feels his soul start quivering in fear and doubt. You can't doubt in the real fake world. "May I speak with you and your husband in private, Mrs. Linscott."

CHAPTER TEN

My Grandfather always said he never wanted to wind up in a nursing home, the exact place where he was fated to enter into and die quickly afterward. He was dead already and maybe we could have saved him by putting a bullet in his head, but we didn't. Instead we let his ninety two-year-old body slowly decay from lung cancer. During the course of any special occasion, be it Christmas or Thanksgiving, he always reminded us of his one wish— to never put him in one of "those places". I think he secretly knew all along that he would die in there.

I didn't bear the responsibility, though, my mother did. I was only sixteen. Too young to be morally responsible for killing someone. That's what she did, she killed him. I wasn't given that responsibility till I was twenty....

Mom didn't have a choice. She had recently been diagnosed with ovarian cancer, I was fourteen, and her mother had passed away—two years after the cab incident. My Grandmother had died in the back seat of that taxicab and she was never the same. I would enter their apartment to the distinct aroma of piss, which seeped into every piece of furniture she sat on and evaporated into the walls and the ceiling. My face cringed, but I never said a word to them about it. I look back and imagine the place with a yellow tinge to it. My grandfather would be sitting on the couch watching the stock exchange or horse racing with the volume on mute. He couldn't hear anyway or at least he pretended he couldn't. For some reason he could always hear me, but never my mother. It got her so mad.

Sometimes he would be asleep, bent over in a white undershirt and khaki pants with a belt. His stomach rose like a giants' and took ages to inflate. He would open one crusted eye if he heard me and then a great smile would spread right across his face. A real smile, like I was the only thing he lived for besides the stock market and horses. "Howdy doody" he'd always say to me and nobody said it like him besides the fact that nobody I knew ever said that anyway. Beyond that, we didn't even need words. I'd immediately pull up a chair and spread out the chessboard across the table. We both knew the drill and he'd sit up and give a loud yawn expelling the sleep from within him. Your greatest friend in the world is the one who you don't even have to say anything to except "Howdy doody."

I'd set up the game, we'd choose who goes first and then he would proceed to beat me as usual. The few words he said came across like a freight train into my head. They would stay there forever because they were planned out, carefully chosen, and contained the wisdom of a man who did not speak unless he had something important to say. "It always pays for experience" he would tell me. They were words that encouraged me to keep playing him even in my deepest frustrations of losing to him every game.

My grandmother was the talkative one up until she got sick. She would sit in a chair next to us and ask me all kinds of questions about how my day was, what I did at school, who my friends were, was I learning and all the other mundane questions that mothers like to ask. She loved to feed me too— "did you eat?" she would ask without waiting for an answer— "I have vegetable soup on the stove and a nice turkey sandwich from the market, would you like any?" She used to make me laugh, and help me to feel comfortable there. I used to spend every New Years with them. Grandma would get all excited about the ball dropping and make comments on how pretty the fireworks were and as soon as the ball dropped grandpa would always stand up and announce that he was going to be the first person to make "a doody" in the new year.

After the accident, though, everything changed. Grandma would stare out into space, say some words I couldn't understand and occasionally piss herself. Her heart had stopped in the back of that cab and now they had a mechanical device called a defibrillator that would send an electric zap to her heart to keep her alive. What the doctors told my parents though, was that it was partly due to her cancer. She struggled in a miserable state for two years before passing away in the hospital bed, holding that brown and tan plush puppy that I had given her. She had a smile on her face and she looked happy holding him. We were going to bury her with it, but someone at the hospital stole all of her stuff while she was lying there. Her earrings, her necklace, and pins that she loved wearing, all gone. They even took the puppy out of the cold arms that were wrapped around him. Maybe it was a Richard or Joseph, laughing all the way down the hallway as they made their escape. We replaced it with a different plush puppy, which made me even sadder.

After my Grandmother's death, her son, (my mother's brother) who I had never seen in my entire life, wanted to have a share of my grandmother's inheritance. However, not seeing my Grandmother for over seven years, she decided to change her will. In rebuke, my uncle called our town police claiming that my mother was holding their father captive against his will. She received the call after one of her chemotherapy sessions.

"WHAT!"

"I'm sorry, Mrs. Linscott, but we're going to need you to come in and prove to us where your father is."

"My father, whom my brother has not seen in over seven years, is in his apartment or at the library where he is welcome to come and go as he pleases. If you don't believe me why don't you go check it out for yourself."

"We're sorry, Mrs. Linscott, but we can't do that. You're going to have to come in."

I'm sitting next to mom in the car when I hear him say this. The poor guy, I think to myself, he's only doing his job. I cringe in my seat in anticipation because I know what's coming.

"What's your name again?" she says very calmly.

"Uh, Charles, but that isn't—"

Imagine the water on your teakettle is beginning to boil and it starts making that low hissing noise, but then escalates to that high-pitched scream. My mom is one tea kettle you don't want to mess with. "Listen to me, CHAR-LES. I'm tired, I'm cranky, I just sat down in a waiting room for four hours and then had chemo for another two. I haven't eaten. I'm driving home with my eyes practically shut to go home and feed my kid. Who's your boss Charles? I want him on the phone right now!

"Uh, he's—"

"Get him on the phone right now! How old are you? How long have you been working as a cop because it sounds to me like you haven't been working there long because you're a complete moron for giving into my brother's CRAP! My brother hasn't been around in over seven years, SEVEN YEARS! You hear me? And you're going to accuse ME of holding MY father under HOUSE ARREST! Get him on the phone! Get him on the phone or I'll make sure you don't have a job by tomorrow morning."

"I think I'll just try and locate your father, okay Mrs.Linscott?"

"Yes, you do that." And she hangs up the phone.

Mom's brother kept filing lawsuits that he never showed up to court for, draining my mother of her energy and finances. Dealing with her own cancer and her father's and then having to be summoned to court brought her will to live down to a new low. This same man I hear was the vice principle of a high school.

It finally ended, but my mom looked even more tired than she used to.

Grandpa was able to take care of himself for a while. He shopped on his own, went to the library often and kept watching the stock exchange, but we could tell he was sad without my grandmother. He lost that energy which once made him light hearted and tell jokes. I stopped visiting as often and we played chess together even less as I became more interested in friends and girls. My mother came down with breast cancer a short time after my grandmother did, but she didn't tell her. She didn't want her to worry or to die with the knowledge that her daughter was ill. She fought it off for a while, but then came down with ovarian cancer. With more chemo it became increasingly difficult for her to look after my grandfather and she feared he couldn't take care of himself for much longer, so she decided to do the only thing she thought she could, which was to place him in a nursing home. He reluctantly agreed to it for he feared my mother's wrath more than death itself. He came down with lung cancer shortly after.

"Son of a gun," my father said. "The man smoked one cigarette every day of his life and I never thought it would catch up to him. We thought he would outlive us all."

I visited him more frequently after that. It took cancer for me to make the time to see him. I watched as his body grew more and more frail. That once great breath of his diminish into short painful gasps. His fingernails turned yellow, his lips dried out and crusted. Those bright green eyes of his, which once had the clarity to focus intently on the chessboard— analyzing pieces, creating strategies, and looking to the future— now only stared off in different directions at once, like they were mere marbles bobbing around in his skull. I fed him the tiniest bit of a grape, but he couldn't even swallow it.

I listened to my mom screaming outside the room, "What do you mean you can't give him more morphine!"

"If we increase the morphine he's going to die even faster."

"Die faster! Do you think this is living? You'll make him die slower and in more pain, for what?"

"There are religious views that we must take into account."

"Religious views! Like what? You don't want to be held responsible for killing him? Listen to me very carefully. He is my father and I choose for him what I think is best. He is dying. You know that. Please, let him die without pain."

The man she's speaking to is quiet for a long time before he let's out a deep sigh, "We'll increase it to ten, but don't ask me for anymore than that. At least not yet."

"Thank you." She turns her back on him and walks off.

I say goodbye to grandpa. No, I say goodbye to the body that is his toxic wasteland. He's not there anymore and I know it's coming soon. I had a swim meet that day and I forgot all about him. I dropped my friend off and was driving down a hill and as I was heading down it I found myself faced with one of the most beautiful sunsets I had ever seen filled with reds and purples. And it was in that moment that it came into view that I remembered grandpa and I suddenly felt the storm coming. A shift and the real world making its way in. A moment later my cell phone rang. I knew before I had even picked it up. My grandfather died in that sunset.

I'll live forever with him in mind. He and my grandmother taught me that pain is worse than death and that dying the way they did is a humiliation that no one should have to endure. It would serve as a good preparation for what was to come.

CHAPTER ELEVEN

Sarah broke up with me. I told her my mother was dying and she broke up with me. It seems to be a common theme. There's a lot more behind that, but I make a small vow to never have a long distance relationship ever again. She was right to end it, it wasn't working, but she was the only steady thing in my life that I had left to hold onto and now it was gone. I think back to the mice and I remember to never love anyone. It helps the tears fall back behind my eyes. "I must think like Richard," I tell myself. "What would Richard do?" I have green eyes, dark green eyes, and Connor has blue. I'm thinking about buying colored contacts.

It just so happens that I was reading *On The Road* by Jack Kerouac on the train ride up to see her, so instead of getting all down in the dumps about it, I decide to grow some balls, say fuck it all to myself, and I pick a girl on the train to sit near. The woman next to me was annoyed that I kept looking at the movie she was watching. It's hard not to look at a moving screen, but whatever, I use it as my excuse to switch seats and you can always tell right off the bat whether a girl is receptive or not.

"Is this seat taken?"

She smiles, "No, not at all." The smile gives it all away and I know I'm in. I take a seat and watch as she moves the bangs of her hair to the side and now I know I could even get laid. Her body is twisted slightly in my direction and I notice that she looks a little young with stark black hair that shines as brightly as her glossy thick lips. She's heavy on the make up, trying to make herself look older with partially penciled in eyebrows and I know I'm dealing with a star. The greatest part about her is that she has green eyes so I know she likes a little darkness.

"I'm Drew."

"Kaleen."

"Nice to meet you, Kaleen. So are you a model or an actress?" This, for the gentleman in the audience, is where you can either bring it all crashing down by scaring them off or impress the shit out of them enough that they're already wet. It's a risky tactic that I don't normally use, but right now I don't give a shit, and when you don't give a shit, suddenly you can become Brad Pitt even if you're not that good looking. Then again, you could also be wrong, in which case you might as well start thinking about cold showers unless you're good at spin control.

"I...I'm an actress. How did you know that?"

"You have a glowing presence about you." In the fake world, you don't tell a girl the truth and by that I mean how you really feel. Not ever. If she looks beautiful you never tell her that, it's another thing that can scare them off. They think you're either a creeper trying to get in their pants or you're already madly in love with them. Even if one is true, you don't want them to think you even give a shit because in the fake world you don't. Best scenario, you tell them you want to be friends even if they look like Helen of Troy. All girls really want is a friend and if they know that friend doesn't want them, then they'll want them. Make them think they're on top and then resist until they put themselves there. Even the fake world can be fun sometimes.

I was never this person. I developed into it. The fake world made me this person, and I hate myself for it. I have to lie about who I am just to fit in and talk to a girl. I have to sell myself like I'm a product. Good job mom and dad. You made a good investment. I'm adaptable to change, I can survive under bad times, but know that cancer is spreading everywhere. It will find its way into the crevices your generation left open.

"So do you want to go to Hollywood?" You've now flattered her and insinuated that she has direction. Put her up high so that she lands in the right place.

"Oh no, no," she blushes. "I like theater. I'd like to be on Broadway someday, though."

"No kidding, you ever been there?" Number two rule, keep conversation away from yourself. This is the fake world, remember, nobody gives a shit about you and if anyone ever asks, you're "good". Being from New York, I'm throwing the line out and hoping she'll grab it. You can talk briefly about yourself, but keep it all on a shallow level. Detail is very important, though. As much as this all seems contradictory, you have to be an on the surface asshole, sweetheart, who can talk and analyze like a woman. If you're contradictory, it means you're interesting. You have to think like a student writing a paper: teachers have hundreds of papers coming across their desks everyday so what makes yours so goddamn special? The goal is to make them stop and take a second glance at it, even if you don't give a shit about the paper or the teacher, you want them to not be bored and to wake up for just a moment and listen enough to land the A that gets you into bed with them. Even Freud knew what he was doing with women.

"Oh, what that means is that you want to get into bed with your father."

"No it doesn't. That's disgusting."

"Then prove it and come over here."

Kaleen's smile gets bigger, "Yeah, I've been there dozens of times. My mom and dad used to take me when I was younger. What about you?"

"I live in New York, but I've only gone to see a few. *Les Miserables* was my favorite second to *Beauty and the Beast* just because I always like the part played by the candle." Now you seem cultured.

"Me too. My favorite is *Cats*. The dancing and the outfits, it's all so fantastical."

"Never seen it, the only part I know is that there are cats involved."

"Yeah, just a couple," she laughs and flips back her hair again. "So that lady you were sitting next to seems a little ridiculous." Now I know that she was watching me and I suddenly feel like Charlie after finding the Golden ticket.

"I think I made her mad from watching her screen."

"What was it?"

"Harry Potter. I couldn't resist."

"She kind of looks like Mrs. Mcgonogal."

"She does now that you mention it. Maybe she tried out for the part and got rejected so she's bitter about it. It would explain her pacing up and down the walkway."

"She's really weird. Is that why you came over here?"

"Well, that, and for other reasons."

"Like what?"

"Like…I wanted more leg room in an isle seat."

"You were in an isle seat."

"Was I?" I look over to the seat I was in before, but it was good enough to avoid the obvious.

"Oh well, so where do you go to school?" This is where you set her up to be in College even if you know she's in high school so it makes them think they look older. You also want to find out just how old they are. I had a teacher in high school— young, somewhere in his 20's— come into class and with no explanation at all, begin telling us about the four year rule. The four year rule being that is it's only considered statutory rape if you're more than four years older. He came in with an actual New York Judicial law book and then copied it on the board:

That means 14-18, 15-19, 16-20, and 17-21. Some dumb ass in the class asked what about if she was eighteen and my teacher called him a dumb ass and said that at eighteen everyone is legal. Then some other dumb ass kid asked what if she was thirteen.

"Look, it just sticks to the four year rule. Do the math James, Jesus. Thirteen goes to seventeen."

"Oh."

Kaleen giggles at me again and she has such a cute giggle. "I'm actually only in high school, but don't hold that against me."

"Oh, so you're—"

"—Seventeen."

"Oh wow, I could have sworn you were at least nineteen."

"Well, how old are you?"

"Nineteen."

"Well, that's not too bad." She giggles again and suddenly I'm hoping no one will ask me to stand up anytime soon.

"So where you headin'?"

"I live with my dad in New Hampshire, but I visit my mom down in Ardsley over the summer."

"Ardsley, no way. I live in Tarrytown."

"We should meet up then. I'll take you into the City."

"You're going to take *me* into the city?" Now I know she likes it on top.

"Yeah, why not?"

"No reason. Sounds fun, where we going?"

"I know a restaurant that my friend works at where we could probably get some drinks."

"So you got connections movie star?"

"You know it."

I'm suddenly aware that her left hand has been twiddling a thin silver necklace with a pearl at the end. This has been going on for the past couple of minutes and I'm unsure if it's a nervous tic or just a habit.

"That's a nice necklace. Where'd you get it?"

"Oh, my boyfriend gave it to me. It was a present for our two year anniversary."

I can stand up now and for you gentleman this is where it's a safe bet to fold in your cards. The fake world is complicated, which is its appeal. Several factors are now at play. One is that she's representing Aces over Kings to you're mid two pair, but because you've made it this far with conversation going the way it has, I'd say she actually has two's over threes, meaning she's still way ahead of you, but there's a chance you can catch you're money card. It all depends on how much you're willing to lose or how much of a scumbag, Richard type you're willing to become. The next thing to be made aware of is that she said two years. Now depending on how long ago that two year gift was, depends on everything because two year relationships are notorious for a break up period. Two years is the benchmark. If you go beyond that, there's a good chance you're going to seal the deal and get married, but if you're unsure, the two-year mark is where you would start thinking about it. Lastly, men, keep your options open. Women always know other women so keep as many friends as possible. If you're a good guy to them, they may even set you up with a friend. This is how it works in the fake world, nobody really knows anybody, but nobody really cares as long as at the end of the day you can get laid. And for you women out there, I apologize for any offenses, and I hold you in much higher regard than the male species, which is why we men have to try so goddamn hard to get inside your heads.

It ended up not working out with Kaleen, although we became friends, but the seed had been planted and now being single, women could become my outlet. Swimming was falling out of my range of sight and I was trying to have my mom disappear close behind it.

CHAPTER TWELVE

I'm not one to quit, but the virus that has been edging its way through my brain is getting stronger. I can't ignore him anymore like I used to. He's a step above annoyance, not quite pain, but enough of a nuisance where I want to reach inside my brain and yank him out. The more I try and think, the worse he gets. I can see him smiling at me as he squirms around my brain cavities continuing to multiply. We have a training trip for swimming once a year where we go down to a place with warm weather to have the most intensive workouts of the season. I remembered the year before, down in Florida, was one of the greatest times of my life, but this year my pace is relatively slow during practice as I wonder what it is that I'm doing here lap after lap, while all the time trying not to think about my mom. I walk into Darth Vader's office.

"Kat, can we talk?"

"Of course, Drew. Have a seat." She has her fake smile on already. "What's up?"

"I can't swim distance anymore. I just can't do it."

"What do you mean?"

"I can do the sets up to 400's (sets of 16 laps), but I can't do anything past that because my mind keeps wandering and you know what's going on with my mom because I'm sure my dad told you."

"He's told me a little, but I'm sure I don't know the full extent of it."

I have to admit, neither do I.

"I think I know what you mean, though," she says. "The longer you're head is under the water the more you start to think about her." She has these moments of clarity, like an Alzheimer's patient remembering a specific detail about an occurrence that happened years ago, but then it all goes away.

"Yes, exactly! I don't know if I'll be able to make it through the training trip because of it."

"We'll just make sure you don't have you do any long distance then, okay?"

"Really? Yeah, that sounds great. Thanks for understanding Kat."

"Anytime." Her fake smile gets bigger.

I walk out of her office, but the conversation reeks of falsity. It's not like her and I make a mental note, placing our talk in the back of my mind in case it needs mentioning again. If it works out, though, I know I'll be able to continue swimming.

***

My head is buried under this blue chlorinated world, holding steady with the black line that makes it's way up and down the pool, never changing, never ceasing to tell me when the end is coming. Oh, Connor, why are you so important to this world of mine? I've been doing this, swimming now, since I was three years old. You've been doing it for how long, three or four years? How can someone care so much for something that's existed in one's life for such a short time? Is this how I feel about you, Connor? Because I know how much you love swimming now and I know you blame me for it. You're falling in love and I'm falling out of it. I'm going to try and explain this to you, Connor, and don't worry, because they'll be trying to tell me the same thing. I'm too young. I don't know anything about what I'm talking about. I'm too young to know that you don't give up on a life so easily. I'm too young to tell people how the world should be working. I'm too young to understand that safe is better and that the world is the way it is for a reason. I'm too young to understand what it is like to have a family and a child that is my responsibility and to want their safety and their happiness. I'm too young to understand that you don't quit, you need to work in this world, and it's a part of life, even if it becomes dull and monotonous. This is what they'll be telling me, Connor, but I'm just going to throw my dad's old words right back at them, "you can be right and still be wrong." Or better yet, I can use their words, "65% correct is still passing." Okay, Connor, now it's your turn.

When you're a little kid you end up repeating certain actions again and again, because your mind finds comfort there. Perhaps you know what I'm talking about, Connor, and perhaps you don't. Have you ever played with the same building blocks for hours and hours? Have you ever played with the same toy dinosaurs for what felt like days when you were a little kid? What about on the playground? I know half the childhood memories I have were on the playground because I never wanted to leave. The adults always get bored and would tell us when it's time to move on. Other times we have to make that decision ourselves. After we've enjoyed the same task for hours on end, we realize that this doesn't take us anywhere. We figure it out. We beat the game and there's nothing left for us to learn. That's why I stopped playing chess with my grandfather, Connor. After enough check mates, you learn the game, you learn the lessons and you had spent time with someone you loved, someone you love still. The adults move on, though. Even grandpa would at some point say, "time for a break" and he'd turn on the stock exchange network or take a nap. This is life. I stopped playing chess with grandpa and I became more interested in girls. Anyone who isn't insane can mark the periods, the ending points in their lives, and they find themselves having to start an entirely new sentence.

Connor, listen carefully. I've beaten swimming. The game is over. Check mate.

I find there is a period coming to my life, an end to a long sentence, and it's coming sooner than it may have because my mother's life is ending. It doesn't mean I can't come back. Even while being interested in girls, I still visited grandpa, maybe not as much, but I still visited. And more importantly, I still loved him. I know you don't understand this, but try and listen. With my head buried under this water, lap after lap, hour after hour, it has become clear that I no longer need this. It has been there for a while now, but it has been mom's illness that's helped to push me over this last barrier. Maybe you'll get faster Connor, maybe I would too, but the results will be the same in my mind. This is where you need my dad's words Connor, "Drew, you can be right and still be wrong." This is where you tell me you're not too young to understand. You tell me I'm psyching myself out. You tell me, swimming is a part of my life, part of *me*, and that you can't see how I can just give up on it. Does this sound familiar to you, Connor? This is where our differences spread wider and wider. My mindset is one way, and yours is another. This is where it becomes impossible for me to explain the guilt, and the terror of losing you, more than my girlfriend, more than any friend in my entire life. I've never had a friend like you, Connor, probably for the same reason that I hate you now. You're telling me not to give up. In a sense, you're the only one left that is encouraging me not to give up on my mother dying.

If you were in my position, I know that you would handle it differently. You would take every doctor who wears glasses and you'd bang those glasses back into their skulls screaming at them to find a cure. I can see you now, taking the doctors by their stethoscopes and holding them by the neck until they have the entire medical staff helping your mother who they've now put in a queen sized medical bed with all the latest and best drugs. Oh, Connor, you're a different kind of Richard. You're the nice kind—with blue eyes and Pantene Pro-V body wash. You wouldn't strangle them, but they would *feel* like they were being strangled, as I feel it now. Because you would make them love you so fucking much, by talking to them till they wanted to help you with all their heart and soul. They'd cure cancer for you Connor and not because you told them too, but because you *asked* them to. Connor, you'd let my sentences run on forever...

Yet, after they cured your mother, you would leave them and never think of them again. You'd erase them. You would no longer love them for what they did. You would forget them like they never were. The car man at the shop cleaned your car and that's all he would ever be to you— a car cleaner. They would become nothing to you as I have become nothing. I've known you for such a short time, but you're my "swimming" when I started at three years old. When I look back on it now, all I can remember is every little thing you did to piss me off, how you piss me off still, and I can't understand why I don't remember anything good about you. Is this how I'm going to remember swimming? Am I going to think of it and only remember Kat who is ruining the sport for me? I feel this way about my mother sometimes too. It's so difficult to remember the good parts of a relationship when it ends badly. The question is, Connor, will I only

remember the bad memories about you? Will I only remember the
bad memories about swimming in this last year? Will I only
remember bad memories about mom?

No, and that is why it's important to look back, to remember,
and to love. Love every scratch and scar on that car of yours.
Sometimes you need to let go and sometimes you need to remember.
When you battle cancer, you know how trivial things are like
scratches on a car. It takes time, but remembering is important.
When mom dies, I need to be able to tell her I'm sorry for all those
times I fucked up—for all the times I wasn't there for her and for
every argument I ever had with her. I need to be able to recall the
faces of every nurse and doctor whoever helped her and I need to
thank them with all my heart. I need to love them, Connor. I'm
drowning myself in alcohol now, but as I said, it takes time. And this
day, I'm ready to remember. I'm you Connor. I really am. You don't
understand that yet, but the only real difference between us is that
I'm dealing with something called fate. The only difference between
you and I Connor, is her. And soon the only difference between you
and her Connor, will be that you're still alive. Don't wait till you're
dead too in order to understand this.

When we arrive at the airport to head out on our training
trip, Connor and his girlfriend Michelle are arguing again and I don't
feel like being a third wheel to it anymore. He's afraid to fly and she

likes to cry so when he's scared, she cries. It's a vicious circle and I'm glad I have headphones with me. Connor and my downfall began with a girl, an extremely special girl, named Dori. As a refresher course, Connor and I are very different, but we like the same women. And as the pattern went, I had pointed Michelle out to him and made him aware that she was attractive and now here they are, boyfriend and girlfriend. In retrospect, I hate the controlling girl with a passion and am glad I didn't get involved with her, but let's start from the beginning.

Dori joined as a freshman the same year as we did. She had bright blonde hair, light freckles, and was slightly chubby. She was kind and genuine and I told Josh and Connor that I thought she was pretty. Of course it didn't come out like that.

"Are you two blind. She is definitely hot."

"I don't know man, she's got a lot of pudge on her," Connor says with a smirk.

"Yeah, but she can lose that."

"Yeah, but still. Even her cheeks are a little puffy, and I'm not really a freckle guy. I like my girls petite." Josh moves his hands in a position like he's holding a girls waist and slapping her ass.

"You two are shallow shits. You can't see past anything."

"Very true," Josh says with raised eyebrows.

"I don't know dude, you're just not selling me on this one," says Connor.

"Whatever."

"It looks like she likes you, though. She keeps talkin' to you."

"She's just nice."

"C'mon man. You should go for it."

I look down to the ground. The real world tells me differently, "I don't think so."

Dori and I became good friends. One day we were left at the lunch table together and out of the blue she started talking to me about her family and friends. Such honesty and trust compelled me to tell her about my life and family. You could enter the real world with Dori and she has blue eyes. My like for her stayed in the back of my mind, but being friends seemed to suit us better. We actually combined forces to get Connor to break up with his first girlfriend from high school: I thought Dori and him would make a far better couple. If I couldn't be with her, I wanted my other half to be.

"Dude, be honest with yourself, you hate her."

"I do not hate her."

"Then why do you never want her to come down to see you?" says Dori.

"I don't know. It's a pain."

"And why is it a *pain* to see your girlfriend."

"What's with the interrogation?"

"You're miserable, man. You are not happy with her; all you do is complain about her."

"I like complaining," Connor laughs.

"Be serious. You fight with her all the time, I hear you on the phone."

"And you never go to see her, she always comes to see you," Dori adds.

"Last time she was on her way here, you were literally yelling and cursing about it. Does that sound like a relationship to you?"

"You don't understand."

"What's to understand? Tell us that you're madly in love with the girl you never want to see and won't even lift a finger for. Tell us. You tell me you love her, right here and now, and I won't mention this again, but I'm banking on the fact that you can't even say it."

Connor looks down at the floor for a long moment then looks up and sees the two of us glaring at him. He smiles, but we stay serious, so then he becomes serious.

"You're right. I don't love her, but let me think about it, okay?"

A few days later Connor broke up with her and he was the best I had ever seen him. We'd be about to go out:

"Oh wait, I think I forgot something," he'd say and pause for a moment. "Oh, nope, nevermind. I don't have to tell someone where I'm going, haha."

It was really great to see Connor not moping. Any girl I knew, I would always introduce her to him, telling her that he was the greatest guy I knew. Connor never went for any of them, though, which I had found odd. It was only during the training trip the year before did he finally make a move.

"Do you find Tara attractive?" I say to Connor in our hotel room.

"No, not at all. Why?"

"I don't know. I think she's got sex appeal."

"She's kind of gross and a little skanky, don't you think?"

"She's not that bad."

"You know how many people she's been with?"

"No, and do you?"

"I guess you're right, you can't judge like that."

"Plus, she's probably really good. Definite sex appeal, I'm telling you."

"Whatever you say, Drew. You going to kiss her when the ball drops?"

"We'll see. I don't think she's really into me."

I wound up hooking up with a girl from a different swim team. I'm about to take her shirt off when she says:

"I'm not sure I can do this."

"Do what? We haven't even done anything yet."

"I know, but I just remembered that I have a boyfriend."

"What, just remembered? How do you just remember?"

"We got together a few days ago."

"Oh...okay."

She pulls me down and we continue to make out for another thirty seconds.

She stops. "I'm sorry."

"That's okay." We keep making out a little longer.

She stops again. So I ask, "Who is he?"

"Oh, he's one of the guys on my team."

I sit up.

"So you mean he's here?"

"Yeah...I'm sorry. I promise I won't tell him."

We stand up and she kisses me one last time. "Thanks."

"Sure." She walks out the door and it closes behind her. "No problem." The first thing I do as she walks out the door is check that my breath is okay. It is and I realize that she's telling the truth. I'd rather it have been my breath.

I come back to the party and Josh comes up to me, "Hey, buddy that was quick." I get a few more, "that was quick" jokes from other people.

"What happened?"

"She turned out to have a boyfriend."

"Ooo, that sucks. So you stopped?"

"Yeah."

"Why?"

"What do you mean, why?"

"Well, you had already made out with her. The damage was done."

I laugh, "I guess I didn't think of it that way. I'll try telling her that next time." I roll my eyes.

"Look," someone says, "the ball is dropping."

I turn to the television:

"4, 3, 2, 1, Happy New Year!" Several of the swim team members turn to each other: some giving hugs, some kissing each other on the cheeks innocently and giggling and the only couple full fledged making out is Connor and Tara. I take a double take and kind of do that head tilt to the side thing like a cockeyed bird and stare at them. I become very confused. I see them leave together and now I'm even more confused.

I'm lying on the hotel bed reading a book when Connor comes in. I look at the clock and it reads two thirty in the morning.

"Have fun?"

"Huh? Yeah." He walks over and sits down on the foot of my bed, looking down at the floor. I don't know whether to say anything, or to keep reading my book. It's obvious he wants to talk or he would have sat down on the foot of his own bed. I decide to give up and look back at my book, but as soon as I do, Connor turns around.

"Do you think Tara is attractive?"

Again, confusion is the right word for the night and I'm wondering if someone fed me Absinth instead of Absolut.

"Yes, remember, I thought she had sex appeal. You alright?"

"Yeah. You don't mind that I hooked up with her, do you?"

I laugh, "No, dude. This is college. If you're not dating, it's a community pool. I didn't think you even liked her though?"

"Yeah. I don't know, it just sort of happened."

"A tongue that far down your throat doesn't just happen."

"Well, I heard a little earlier in the night that she was planning on trying to hook up with me."

"What happened to Beth? I thought you wanted to hook up with her."

"I did. I don't know."

"You think you're going to hook up with her again?"

"I don't know."

I laugh again, "Alright, dude."

"It's just that...I don't know."

"Listen, it's not like you're dating her or anything. Did you at least get something out of it?"

"She gives a really good blow job."

"Well, for now, that's all that's really important. Get some sleep. We'll talk about it when your other head is on straight in the morning."

I didn't know it then, but this became a common routine. Later in the year, he ended things with Tara because him and Dori were becoming closer. She had lost that weight she had on at the beginning of the year.

Connor and I are eating lunch in the cafeteria when he pops the question:

"Do you think Dori and I would be good together?"

The food that was about to enter my mouth misses and falls off my fork onto the tray. I look up, then look back down at the fallen piece of food and try to scoop it back up again. "Yeah, I actually think you two would be great together. You talk to each other all the time and Tara isn't really right for you anyway. All you two do is have sex. You could have an actual relationship with Dori."

"So you think I should go for her?"

"Do what you want. Do you have feelings for her or not?"

"Yes, I do."

"Then go for it. It's not that complicated and she's obviously into you."

"You think?"

"You're like a blind dog without a nose. Yes, she's into you Romeo, now go woo her like you do best. You know, the only reason girls are into you is because you're so goddamn oblivious. They all think it's the cutest thing."

He laughs at this, "I don't know, I just talk to them I guess."

"That's right. You talk to them without even the hint of wanting anything from them like you're talking for talking's sake and they love that. It's a patience thing, which I don't have. I don't really care to talk to a person I don't know or like, but you appear to like everyone, when it's really you who doesn't care. You just like to talk."

"I guess. It's not like I don't care though."

"Whatever, if it works, keep it up. I'm not going tell you to change."

Connor and Dori hit it off quite well, the problem was that I started to see less and less of the both of them. I heard that all Connor was doing after practices was lying in Dori's bed for hours at a time. It became that the only time I would see him was at workouts. At first, I didn't take it as anything more than him getting involved in a relationship, but I wasn't sure. A month later, after only seeing him at practices, he resurfaced. He simply appeared in my room with tears in his eyes.

"Oh Jeeze, you alright?"

"Can we talk?"

"Yeah, of course."

"Let's go to the common room."

I look at the clock. It reads 1:00am. It might be empty.

"OK."

We both take seats. Connor is looking down at the floor, bent over his knees with his hands clapped together; he's rocking slightly. There's silence for a long time.

"Dori broke up with me."

"I'm sorry." More silence. "So what happened?"

"You know that thing that happened with Stephanie awhile back, right?"

"Which thing? You mean the time you kissed her while you still had a girlfriend?" Stephanie is a long time friend of Connor's from his hometown who he has always had a crush on. When he was with his old girlfriend from high school, he ended up kissing her on a night that they were both drunk together.

"Yeah, it apparently became a real issue with Dori. Everything was going fine, and she thinks that once a cheater, always a cheater, and it was the fact that I lied about it that also gets to her."

"Why would you even tell her something like that?"

"It kind of just came up and I didn't think it was that big of a deal because it was in the past and I felt bad about it, but it's like because of this one thing I can't be with her and it's ridiculous."

"Yeah, that does sound a little ridiculous. I mean you only kissed her, right?"

"We made out for a little while, but we were both drunk, and we were on the beach and it was only that one time. I even stopped myself."

"I can here Dori's voice already, "That's not an excuse.""

"Yeah, that's what she said alright."

"Jeeze, talk about your past coming back to haunt you."

"Tell me about it. I can't get it through my head why it's the biggest deal in the world. Because I...I...I love her, and I wouldn't do something like that now."

"Well, you still like Stephanie don't you?"

"Yes, but I've developed real feelings for Dori."

"And did you tell her that?"

"Yeah, but she doesn't want to hear it. I told her I'd even not see Stephanie anymore to keep us together."

"And what did she say?"

"She said that would be the last thing she wanted me to do. It made it even worse because then she became upset that I would up and leave a best friend like that. When I didn't really mean it that way."

"Well, you shouldn't have said that, but I do know what you mean. You were just trying to make a point."

"Right. She takes everything I say so literally and I don't know what to do. It would make so much more sense if we broke up over something else, but this is so stupid."

"I'm sorry, dude."

"I'm losing it. Every time I think about her, it's like I start to go crazy and what's worse is my roommate is over at her place talking with her so I gotta see him leave the room and it's all more than I can take...Don't tell anyone this, okay, but...I...I've been thinking about committing suicide."

My head shoots up. "What!?"

"I keep having thoughts in my head like jumping off a bridge or something like that. I don't know what's going on, I don't understand this. Things were going so well. I don't want to live with myself if I can't be with her."

"Okay, Connor look at me, and I need you to listen to me very carefully, alright. Look at me. You've been dating this girl for a month and I know it hurts, but suicide is ridiculous. Look at yourself. Look at all that you've got going for you. I mean, come on, I'm jealous of you half the time with how you are with women and trust me if it doesn't work out with Dori it's because it *wasn't meant to be*. It hurts right now, but give it three weeks and you'll be feeling better. You might even meet a girl you like more than Dori and then trust me it's like Dori will be completely forgotten about. You have to put things in perspective because I'll kill you before I let you commit suicide."

Connor laughs with a tear in his eye.

"Listen, this is what we're going to do, alright. We're going to go balls deep opposite end of things and have a complete girls night. I'm going to buy us some ice cream and chocolate and we're going to pig out and watch a movie and get your mind off this because the more you think about her the worse it's going to be. How does that sound?"

He laughs a little, "That sounds alright, I guess."

So we pigged out and ate ice cream, and talked the guy talk of "Did you at least get anything out of it?" and all that crap that makes people feel better and within a month he was.

The next girl was Natasha, a girl who I had made out with and never really spoke to again till a few months later. We kept as friends through an online medium, but it was mutually not reciprocal romantically and we had no face to face contact. So when I ran into her again and introduced her to Connor, he asked me what had happened.

"She smelled."

"What do you mean she smelled?"

"I don't know how else you describe it. She had an odor to her that I didn't like, you know, like the whole pheromone thing was not attractive to me, but she's a really nice girl and if you want to go for her, I'd have no problem with it. She's really easy to talk to."

"What do you mean, though, by she smelled?"

"I don't know, find out for yourself. Maybe you'll find it more attractive, it was like a pungent foreign type odor. You know how like some blacks or Indians have an odor to them, well she had an odor."

"She's not Indian, though."

"Dude, you know what I mean. I'm sure I have an odor too, I've just been living with myself for so long I'm probably used to it."

So Connor hooked up with her.

"I don't smell anything, dude," he said upon coming back from her place.

Connor was with Natasha for a few months, but it came back to that time where he asked me for advice.

"I don't know if I should stay with her over the summer or not."

"Why not?"

"Because, what's the point."

"Well, do you like her?"

"Yeah, I like her."

"Do you really like her?"

"I don't know."

"Listen, it comes down to the same thing with you. If you think it's going to go somewhere then stay with her and if you don't then don't. You have no problem being miserable forever."

"I don't see the point of breaking up with her if there's no reason to."

"Then deep down, you're being a selfish asshole because a girl stays with you until she either, one, finds another guy that she likes more than you, or two, because she wants to eventually marry you. Girls always want to know where things are going and if you don't love the girl than you should keep your options open OR you should play the woman card and keep seeing her till you find someone else you like more."

"That sounds like the dumbest thing I ever heard."

"Yeah?"

"Yeah, but I think I'm going to go with the woman card. That sounds like it will work out."

"So how's your summer going?"

Connor ended things with Natasha so he could begin things with his present girlfriend Michelle. After all this time, with Connor not being interested in any other girls, it took till this time for me to finally put the pieces together. He only goes after the girls I tell him I like or find attractive.

Our relationship had come down to more than seeing eye to eye on certain issues, it became that the only judgment call he could make was one that I supported. If I liked a girl, it must mean there was something there that he simply didn't see right away. Maybe my love for him had distracted me from what was clearly a serious issue, but he always showed potential for change and growth. Connor was smart when he wanted to be and could always see the other side of an issue, except when it came to girls. Everything was coming to a head and my mom forced me to see people for the way they were including a new look at myself. Connor was going to attach himself to Michelle like he did with Dori and lock himself up in a dungeon with her. This was going to happen and I would have to prepare myself for the inevitable yet again, except this time I needed someone more than ever.

My head is now buried under the water of this pool. Too many churning thoughts and emotions keep swelling up. I'm losing my friends, I'm losing my family, and I'm losing swimming. I keep trying, but the real world keeps telling me to stop. I try again, but it tells me to stop. I try yelling back at it, but it's beating me. I'm going to lose, but losing doesn't matter. Fighting matters.

CHAPTER THIRTEEN

The three-year-olds had it right all along. We should have stuck to saying, 'no' to everything.

"No." I say to Darth Vader after I stop at the wall.

"No. What do you mean no?"

We finished a warm up that was a hundred laps long and now she's asking us to do a set of four 800's, which is four sets of thirty-two laps, which is *another* hundred and twenty-eight laps and I want to scream. I did that first 400 with my head buried under the water, and I felt the itching stronger than ever. It wants out. I tried to shake it off, but I can't any longer.

"I won't do it, Kat."

"You mean you can't do it?"

"No, I just refuse to do it. We talked about this."

"Talked about what?"

I want Luke Skywalker to jump out of nowhere and slice her head off with a light saber. It would still have that dumb naïve smile attached to it even as it rolled into the water.

"About me not doing anything over 400's."

"Well you're only doing a couple of 800's, the rest is broken up." What she means is, there are only two sets of 800, with a five second rest, two sets of 400, which I know I won't even make the rest for, and then four sets of 200, which I also won't make the rest for. I give her my death stare.

"It's practically four, 800's, Kat."

"So you're not going to do it?"

"No."

"I can't believe this. You can't not do the set."

"Yes, I can."

Picture saying no to your boss at work. He's got that angry look in his eye and you have that mandatory such and such thing due that you don't give a shit about for that entire job that you don't give a shit about. Maybe you never even gave a shit and once upon a time this was only temporary and suddenly it pops into your head that you can always say no. "No." Your boss screams and screams and screams, but all you can think about is the child you have at home or your spouse and how you won't have the money to live or afford your apartment or the nice house you have anymore. We forget as human beings how we once had the ability to take the land and build a home, anywhere – no property taxes. If we needed food we could pick an apple off a tree, we could hunt a wild animal. No bills, no taxes, no property rights, no lawyers, just the land and a place to build. I once heard this story about a fisherman who caught one fish every day out in the Ocean. He had a small place on the shoreline and one day he was approached by a tourist who watched as the man reeled in a large fish.

"Wow, that's incredible. Do you catch those all the time here?"

"I suppose so."

"How many do you catch?"

"Just one."

"Just one! A day?"

"Yeah."

"Well, why don't you get a bigger boat and get some more rods, then you could catch three a day."

"Don't need three and don't want to use up all the fish."

"I know if I had fish like this where I lived I would catch as many fish as I could and make my own company," The man said. "Then I'd get even bigger boats and be able to catch more fish. I'd be rich."

"And what would you do with all that money?"

"I don't know. I suppose I would go buy a place by the beach where my family and I could live."

"Well, I already have that." And the man smiled.

Take everything you have. Take it all. Pack it up good. Go sell that China that you have stored up, the ones you've been saving for those guests that never came. They're too special to be used and somehow you think the president of the U.S. will one day wind up at your doorstep and you can finally use all that China. You've got fifty-four plates of China with twenty-three teacups and all the same little flowery designs on all of them. You have six large salad bowls and thirty-seven teacup holders. So you wind up having more bowls for salad than you have salad in the fridge, more teacup holders than you have tea glasses all together, and fifty-four plates for your three person family and the president of the United States who you will be serving frozen macaroni and cheese to. You wind up taking those kinds of guests out to a restaurant.

She called me. Mom did. A couple of days ago. I hear the ringing and in a daze I check who is calling. I look at the clock and it reads four in the morning. Apparently these late hours make for the best conversation.

"Hello."

"Drew. Drew are you awake?"

"Yeah, yeah, mom, is everything alright?"

"Yes, I have something really important to tell you."

"What? Yeah, sure, what's going on?"

"There's China in the house."

"What?"

"China."

"CHI-NA?"

"Yes, the China."

"What's China?"

"There's glass China, plates, bowls and other glass items. You need to promise me that you won't throw it away."

"Throw what away?"

"The China."

"Is this what you called me about?"

"You need to promise me that if I die you won't throw it away."

"Mom, this is ridiculous, it's four o clock in –."

"—promise me. Okay?"

"Yeah, mom, sure. I promise I won't throw away your China."

"Thank you. It may not mean something to you now, but it will someday. You don't understand now what it means and I know you don't care. So promise me."

"Okay, mom, I promised already. I won't throw away the China."

Fifty-four plates, twenty-three teacups, thirty-seven teacup holders, and six salad bowls, all of which I haven't seen any of in my whole life. I'll be packing it all up after she dies and those guests never came. That's why I'm telling you to pack it all now or sell it. Get rid of all of it, quit your job, and go live in a place on the water where you can catch a few fish a day to feed your family. You slave all day for your child to have an education, at the end of which, he or she can't even say a two-letter word, "No."

I say it again to Kat, "No, I won't do it." What's the point of working to have health insurance if you're already dead inside.

CHAPTER FOURTEEN

My shoulder blew out soon after that and Jessica, my therapist, said it could have been psychosomatic, meaning my mind influenced my body the way it wanted. I wanted to stop swimming.

I tell Jessica I've been having bad dreams, really bad dreams. She asks of what, and I say I don't know. I only remember being chased and going through places that look like an evil Doctor Seuss book. I tell her that when most people hit the climax of their dream, they wake up and I don't. I keep dreaming. She asks what the climax is.

I see me. I see the gun.

I tell her it isn't what it seems like.

I see me. I see the gun, silver and gleaming from a non-existent light. I see me pointing the gun at my head.

I tell her in the dream I'm committing suicide.

I hear the click of the trigger. I hear a loud bang.

She asks me if I want to commit suicide.

I hear laughing.

I stare off into the distance.

I hear laughing.

No, not consciously, I tell her, but it scares me that I do unconsciously.

I see me. I see my brains splattered everywhere, red and purple with nerve endings still squiggling around, but I'm still alive. I hear laughing.

She says its okay and asks again if I'm sure that I have no conscious thoughts of suicide and I say I'm positive. I tell her I'm still scared, though.

I see an older man walk up to me and take the gun away. He's smiling. I have a hole in my head and he's smiling.

She tells me that my mind is trying to find ways out of the situation I'm in.

I turn and run and he laughs. The laughter fades, but I know he'll find me.

She tells me I have anxiety. She offers me some anti-anxiety medication that she will set up with the psychiatrist and tells me I need to stop drinking.

"I can't stop drinking."

"Why?"

"I can't sleep without a beer at night."

"It won't help with your bad dreams."

"But then I can't sleep."

"The anti-anxiety medication will help with that, but you can't drink with it. Even if you don't take it, I still don't want you drinking because the medicine needs time to get into your blood stream."

I start to shake at the thought of not being able to sleep.

"Okay, I'll try it."

"How have your alcohol classes been going?"

"They say I'm not allowed to talk about it."

"You can talk about it here. Nothing leaves this room."

The walls, the talking, the chasing; I'm locked in my mind and I can't get out. Nothing leaves this room.

I take a deep breath.

We enter the classroom with mostly kids from college and a couple of high-schoolers. We're all laughing and joking around. Two of the kids in the room are a month shy of their 21st birthday and another was only a few days away from her 21st birthday when she got caught for underage drinking. She is twenty-one and a few months now.

It's a joke. All of it is. And they want to make it serious. I saw one of the instructors finish her cigarette before coming into the room, she still smells of it. I wonder if she was eighteen when she started. She has this serious look on her face, similar to the rapist cop who got me. It's that same look, like they know something that I don't, so they show me.

They put up a slide show of all the images you can think of where people were drunk driving. Limbs in different places, bodies torn in half, heads decapitated, scarred faces, burnt faces and every face has the face of my mother: her missing eyes, her charred black flesh, her head through a glass windshield.

None of the kids in here were caught for drunk driving. None of the kids in here spent the night in jail because this was the state's alternative for us after that incident at the blue house plus a nice donation of 300 dollars. I asked the lawyer if she thought it was better than fighting the case and she said yes. She said I wouldn't win. I guess nobody can have a nice congenial and rational conversation in court.

They bring this smart kid in from prison, Jimmy, to tell us how he's cleaned up. He tells us how he was an alcoholic, but he was also just a terrible kid who smashed in car windows and set fires to houses. I've never done any of those things. Jimmy tells us about how prison isn't fun and how we should do our best to stay in school. We all say, "Thank you, Jimmy," and Jimmy leaves.

They show us a fire engine and a hospital vehicle. They tell us all about how much each costs: how much it costs to carry our bodies, how far they stick the catheter up our penis', how much it costs to use the CPR unit, how many people die from drunk driving accidents. They tell us stories of their rescues about removing people's skin from seats with a scissors, about kids flying fifty feet through the air and into a tree leaving the bottom half of themselves behind. They tell us of this guy who passed out in his shower with the hot water on and when they found him his skin was melted off. He kept complaining about how cold he was and they could barely lift him up without his skin dripping off their hands. The rescue person knew he would be dead before he got to the hospital.

They don't want me to tell you these things, though. They only tell us, the kids who drink illegally probably because we know these things already. Don't they know it's why we're drinking in the first place?

This is their legalized form of *Clockwork Orange*, because we signed a piece of paper saying we wouldn't say anything or else we would go to jail, but I'm only telling this to my therapist so it's okay...

They want to make us sick so that we won't drink anymore, so that we become good little members of society, so that when our bosses drive us into the ground, and we work the monotonous job for the next sixty years of our lives, we'll never say the two-letter word, "no". There's too much bad stuff out there so stay away from it.

Drinking is bad. That is why we celebrate the greatest writer's and some of the greatest alcoholics we've ever known: Hemmingway, Shakespeare, Faulkner, F. Scott Fitzgerald, Stephen King, Edgar Allan Poe, Jack Kerouac and Oscar Wilde among many others. Should I go through the artists: Van Gogh, Picasso, Modigliani, Pollack. How about the great leaders: Churchill and Grant. How about the religious figures? Moses and Jesus. Am I mistaken or did we not learn about these great individuals in school? How many hours did we slave over their work and how many grades did we receive under the "A" mark because we didn't measure up to *them*? We didn't drink and drive. We were in a house drinking around friends who watch out for each other, going only a little out of the boundaries, but still being safe; like driving the car backwards, but stopping at every stop sign and staying under the speed limit. Maybe you're still not getting it.

I remember watching television when I was little; I think it may have been a babysitter who sat me down in front of it. Whoever it was, she told me not to move. She told me I could get in real trouble if I moved. She explained to me that if I moved around, or left her sight, I could get really hurt. "You don't want to get hurt, do you?" She said. "No," I replied. I understood hurt. I understood pain. That's when you get your head smashed through the front windshield or you pass out in a hot shower and your skin melts off or having your body hit a tree at forty miles an hour. I've had nothing leading up to this pain, because I've been placed in front of a television set and I haven't moved for years. For twenty years now I haven't moved.

This is why their scare tactics will work because this type of pain seems more than anything we could ever endure with our perfected televised self-images. Even with my mother dying, I see it all in pretty pictures, and outside of myself. Life is starting to break its way in though because Death is breaking in. I'm shaking for the first time. The schools have been avoiding it, trying to keep us safe because the parents kept complaining, the lawyers had to make their voices heard so they could make money and all the while they never stopped to ask us what we, the kids, wanted. So instead of pretty pictures we read pretty words from a book in which the teachers expect us to sit still for hours and not move. They expect us to memorize the names of people who they later tell us may have never even existed and who we shouldn't become. They want us to learn all of this to keep us safe so that we may learn the system to keep the future generations safe.

Yet who are the ones they ask us to become, but the ones who lived great lives from going out of their safe boundaries. The ones whose poems came from hearts filled with despair or love. Not the kind of love on a television set, but the kind where you love so bad it hurts. The way I loved that duck while it was still an egg, the way I loved the mouse, the way I loved grandma and grandpa, the way I love mom, but they never prepared me for losing them. Nobody really dies in television.

When that duck's head fell over to its side and it lay there dead, the teacher should have said, "Drew, this is death. This is what happens when you die, and it's okay. It was okay to love him and it's okay if it hurts. It will make you stronger, and you will love again and you will hurt again and that's okay. You won't be afraid to go out and live because you'll know that you will die too. I repeat, you will die

Drew, but it's better to have been like this duck who at least tried his hardest to break out of that shell to live. He died trying to live, Drew, and that's all that matters."

I learn about the great men of history, the Alexanders and the Napoleons, and all the other Richards, but I watch as they tell Richard to behave and put him on suspension. They tell Richard that he won't get into a good school if he doesn't behave himself and that if he doesn't go through school he won't amount to anything. Richard gives them the finger and storms out. I watch Richard do all this from behind my television set as I sit placidly in my desk chair watching the teacher's reaction. I hate Richard, but I envy his defiance and his willingness to walk out of the classroom. Nobody ever told me that I could just walk out. No, I had to read that in a book where Holden Caulfield ups and leaves the school. They tell us this is a classic, but don't drink kids, that's bad. Don't skip class or we'll punish you.

After all they've taught us they rip it away. They tell us to not be creative, not to be smart and not to branch out. I thought there would be a time when school would end, but no, they've extended it to the law as well. Well, fuck them all. Put all their heads through glass windows and watch them shatter to pieces. I want to buy the largest blender on the face of the fucking planet and put them all in it with all their money and all their laws and I want to blend them into oblivion along with all my memories.

I want to take these instructors out back, with all the cops, with all the judges, and all the lawyers with their cigarettes and with their, "Let's go to the bar after this," and I want to take them and show them all the images in my head. I want to shove it all down their throat and then curse every plague of it on them. They don't know me, but they pretend to, so if you're listening, let me show you what's in my head, if you're listening let me show you about cancer, about life, and about death. Let me show you what's on the dark side of the moon.

CHAPTER FIFTEEN

Her legs are open, her body beautiful and moving sensually up and down. Her curves, her breasts, and everything is flowing in this black and white world. The scene comes with the approach of an ominous storm and I see glimpses of light and shades of gray, but it's so quiet that it calls to me like death itself. Rain flows through my hair and into my skull. I feel alive. She has no head and no face and her belly is beginning to enlarge. I hear it crying before I even see it. The stomach gets bigger and bigger, the belly button widening. It grows like a watermelon being filled with air until it can't possibly grow anymore.

It pops out with the umbilical cord still attached to it covered in black blood. It's screaming. I see a flash of light, followed by the loud crack of thunder. The mother's body goes limp. I don't care about her. I only care about myself and the baby.

The baby is pure white, but dripping black, with black eyes like strands of cobwebs sealed with more blood. It's wailing and wailing right at me. The rain glistens on its pale skin with the black blood still dripping off him like a white whale thrust out of a sea of oil. It stands up on two stumpy legs and starts running after me. I leave the faceless woman's dead body to run across rooftops and across long grass fields. Everywhere I go I hear whaling and a trail of black blood for hours and hours. I run until I grow tired and can't run anymore. I turn slowly, shivering with fear and from the cold sweat that has drenched itself over my half naked body. I hear his presence echoing off the walls of steel buildings from far way. I feel his weight pressed into the ground, sucking me into him like gravity.

I stand face to face with the tiny demon, but it takes me a second before I open my eyes. It's breathing heavily and staring at me with its sealed black eyes. Its chest moves up and down furiously as it catches its breath. Its little arms, strong and steady, hang out by its sides like a cowboy ready to draw. I can't move and am forced to look at it breathing and staring, completely eye level with him. He smiles and I'm scared as its mouth opens to sharply pointed teeth and he leaps onto my neck with a quick burst of speed and clamps down hard and stiff as a vice. The pain shoots its way through the entire right side of my body. I hear him cackling as I wake up.

I'm breathing heavily, and full of sweat. My hand moves to my neck where the bite mark was and I look over.

"You alright?"

"Yeah, yeah, I'm fine."

"You don't look okay."

She's blonde with small perky breasts, and she's sitting up next to me, her naked body taking me by surprise. She touches my shoulder gently and I can't remember her name.

"Yeah, I'm alright. What, what time is it?"

"It's 9:30."

"I got to go."

I tell Jessica about the dream and what I think.

"I've been fooling around a lot and I think it's starting to get to me. I'm trying to take my mind off of mom and I guess women seem to be my outlet, but I'm not like this. Everything is intensified. These aren't normal dreams."

"What do you think the baby means?"

"I don't know, maybe fear of getting a girl pregnant. She doesn't have a face, so it's like I don't care about who she is. It could represent fear of disease."

"And how about you being chased by it?"

"I guess that the decisions I'm making now are going to come back to haunt me. Something like that. Maybe I believe that I can't run from this and what's going on and what I'm doing."

"What about the black blood?"

"Again, probably disease or darkness."

There's a long pause as she calculates her next words, "How about cursed?"

"Cursed? What do you mean cursed?"

"Think about it."

I think about it and I can't possibly understand what that means. Why would my child be cursed? Because of who I am? Because of all this? Because I feel like I'm going crazy?

"I don't know. I can't think of anything."

"Did you ever think that maybe the baby is you?"

The floor just fell out from under me. "Me?"

"Think about it. What would that mean?"

"I don't know." I think about it. I'm born with black blood and I'm running; there is the faceless mother that I don't want to see or recognize and she's dead after I'm born; there are the closed eyes and facing it at eye level and it suddenly dawns on me what she wants me to say.

"Wait, what!? You think I'm cursed?"

"No," she says quietly, her hand pensively resting against the side of her chin, "but I think you do."

***

I think I'm cursed and I don't know what to think. Everyone's dying and I must think I'm cursed. I'm walking back to my dorm when I hear my cell phone ring and I ignore it.

I don't think I'm cursed. I've had a good life. I am simply going through a rough patch, one that eventually everyone must take and I'm taking it a little earlier than most. I need to breathe.

I breathe.

The phone stops ringing. I wonder if Kara is still in my room...Oh yeah, that's her name, Kara. She's a nice girl, and I'm an asshole because I don't love her. I can't love her, because I can't really love anyone. I try to feel, but it's useless. It always feels like it won't work out, so what's the point.

The phone starts ringing again and I'm annoyed because I want to think about the dream and what Jessica said. I look at the phone and the caller I.D. says it's from Dad. I've been trying not to feel and suddenly the real world sends a shiver up my spine. I answer it.

"Hello?"

There's a pause.

"Hey, Drew, are you there?"

"Yeah, dad."

"Drew, I put your mom in the hospital again, I didn't know what else to do."

"What do you mean, what's wrong?"

"She wants to die, Drew."

"What do you mean she wants to die?"

"She wants to kill herself; she's actually been trying to kill herself."

"What, how?"

"It's okay, she's back in the hospital and they're looking after her and trying to keep her out of pain, but I don't know how long they'll keep her there."

"Dad, I don't know what's been going on. I don't know practically anything. Has her tumor gotten bigger, what's been happening? You don't tell me anything?"

"Her tumor is inoperable. There's nothing they can do, but that's not bothering her as much as her rectum is. She can't go to the bathroom, and she can't eat. She's on the bowl screaming. All she can eat is baby food. She's been screaming that she wants to die."

"Well, should I come home? I should definitely come home. Can I come home?"

"No, your mother and I want you to stay in school. You can't re-take the semester."

"What if I could take a small leave? We have our spring break in a couple of weeks, I might be able to take the next couple of weeks off and do the work from home. That'll give me three weeks with mom."

"Well, if you think you can do it that would be great. I'm sure your mother would love to see you."

"I need to come home, Dad. I'll find out what I can do."

"Alright, Drew, I'll talk to you later."

My only communication with them for months has been coming in over the phone and I'm sick of it. I don't know what's going on and everything has been guess work and thinking and imagining. My mother wants to kill herself and I don't blame her.

Jessica had mentioned that I could take a leave if I needed to and I'd been hesitant to, but now it seemed necessary almost like I was being called, like the puzzle was falling into place and I was falling with it into the picture like the moment before a storm and everything is finally so clear.

I tell Jessica that there has been something I've been hiding from her. There is something I don't tell people because they usually don't understand such things. When I was little I believed in things a lot longer than all of my friends. I didn't stop believing in Santa Clause till I was thirteen, I still believed the tooth fairy was leaving me money up to losing my last tooth, I believe in stories about extra terrestrials and mythical creatures. *Where the Wild Things Are* is where I have always been. I took rides with *Danny and the Dinosaur* till I learned how to drive a car. I've sworn to have seen ghosts, experienced their presence, or at least believed enough that I could have. I've found myself moving chess pieces off the board to squares that don't exist and I've woken up in the middle of the night and found myself with tears in my eyes for no reason that I knew of. I've dreamed of things that I have never seen and I have to believe above everything else that my mother isn't going to die because I've been told that I'm the only one who can save her.

I tell Jessica that I have this problem that I never know where to start.

I was ten years old when I heard my parents fighting. I can't tell you what it was about, but I remember it being a frequent thing. I had a friend, Ben, whose parents had a divorce and I wondered if that could happen to me. He acted like he was fine, but I could see that he wasn't and I didn't want to be like that.

We have this wooden staircase with white walls on the sides and exactly thirteen steps. I once heard that thirteen was an unlucky number so I would always try to skip one step to make it twelve. I had a dream that I stood at the top, looking down and I tried to take a step, but instead I flew. I landed gently at the bottom and opened the front door when a quiet voice came into my head.

"Drew."

I stop.

"Drew, where are you going?"

My dream world opens up to the real one and I realize I'm trying to leave my house. "Where am I going?" I say to myself. I look at my arms and I have small bruises that weren't there before, but I feel fine. I go back upstairs and go to sleep.

We're all just waking moments in time till the next waking moment.

My mother is sitting down crying on the third step. Apparently I have woken up and I find myself in dinosaur pajamas. This is real. This will make a memory.

My dad is nowhere to be found. I don't know what to do.

I walk over and face her from the bottom of the stairs and I think about how three is a lucky number. She's balling her eyes out, all alone, and I want to cry with her. I sit down next to her and hold her in my arms. I don't say a word. I just sit and hold as the minutes pass until she calms down a little. She looks up and smiles and through broken tears she speaks.

"I don't hate him...your father. He can sometimes make me really upset is all." She goes back to crying for a few minutes before calming down again.

"He doesn't understand sometimes and he yells. I can't take his yelling at me. You're such a good kid, Drewster. Whatever you do, try not to make a girl cry in this world. Not like this. You're going to have so many girls chasing after you." She laughs at this, and I can see her tears diminishing, but then she stops and a serious look comes across her as if the whole world has stopped.

"I'm going to die young, sweety. I know it. I've known it my entire life."

"What? Don't say that mom."

"It's okay. I know it and it's okay."

"You don't know that."

"I do."

"No, I'll protect you." I grab her a little bit tighter than before. "I won't let you die."

"Thanks sweety." She gives me a look like she knows it's not true, but she wants to believe in me. "And thank you for making me feel better." She starts crying again. "Mommy needs to be alone right now, okay?"

"Okay."

The real world makes exceptions sometimes, but I haven't figured out how. My mother telling me that she was going to die young might mean merely an expression of fear to some people, but coming from her, it meant something far more. Her abilities were of no surprise to me at that point, and I knew that when she said something was going to happen, it usually did. Some people would classify it as being psychic, but she preferred the term, "sensitive." Sensitive to the real world and in touch with the universe in ways we could never even imagine. I am not a sensitive, but my mother made me sensitive to the real world's existence. I am convinced that we are all sensitive in this way, it just depends on how well we listen – or believe.

When I was a baby, she told me she would try to see if I had the gift by giving me little tests. She would wait till I'd be sleeping in the middle of the night and she'd be lying up in bed awake. She said she'd send me messages and I would wake up crying. She said she did this several times and it worked every time. My dad put an end to it when he found out she was doing it especially because she'd wake him up and make him put me back to bed. She was happy about this and she said there was more to it than testing me. She said she was creating a bond in me at a young age, from me to her. Something that could make us aware of each other, something she said she could protect me with. It would connect us mentally. What she could save my life with, would also set up the agony for when we would be torn apart.

The first time she saved my life, I was two years old. My mother woke up in the middle of the night and told my father that I was going to drown. We were in Florida, she said, and dad brought me into the ocean when a strong current took him and I went under the water. The last thing she saw was him letting go of my hand. Then she woke up. My dad was a non-believer and he told her that she was overreacting and that even if we did wind up in Florida, which he said wouldn't be happening anytime soon, that there was no way he would bring me out in the ocean far enough where I could be swept away.

Two weeks later we got the phone call and I heard the screaming happening upstairs.

"We're not going."

"We can't not go. What am I going to tell my parents?"

"Tell them we don't have the time."

"But we've been needing a vacation anyways and they're offering to pay for the whole thing."

"Don't you remember anything of what I said?"

"Yes, okay, but that's not going to happen."

"It is going to happen! You don't listen to me! We're not going and that's final."

"What if I promise you that I won't take him into the water."

"I don't trust you."

"Why not?"

"Because I'm married to you is why not! You think I'm stupid?"

"No, but I promise on this one, honey. If I don't take him into the water than it can't happen, right?"

No response.

"Right?"

"Yes, but if we don't go at all than I know it can't happen."

"Can't you trust me?"

"I can trust you. But first you have to say it."

"Say what?"

"Say that you believe me. I want to hear you say it."

"Why do I have to say it?"

"Because I know you don't believe in it."

"Is that what this is about?"

"Just say it, William."

"Okay...I believe," He sighs, "I believe you, EVEN THOUGH, I know it won't happen. Even if you're right, it won't happen, because I'll make sure he's alright."

"He goddamn better be and that's all I have to say about that."

"What's that supposed to mean?"

She walks out of the room.

Once down in Florida, we all went down to the beach with my grandparents. Mom's stubborn reminder continued to my father about not letting me go near the water. Dad and I played with the sand making great castles and digging up trenches. Mostly it was him showing me all of this while I giggled and poured water into a toy mill.

I watch as dad looks over and notices that mom's asleep. He asks me if I want to go into the water, but I don't really know what he's talking about. He takes me by the hand and leads me to the edge.

The water is beautiful as it inches up onto the shore and then gently recedes. The white foam residue creeps up near my toes and I put one toe in and pull it back out and giggle.

Dad tells me it's okay and he puts both his feet in while looking down at me to do the same. The sky is a pristine blue and fades off into brighter shades as it is engulfed by the sun stretching its light into every crevice of the waves and heating the sand beneath our feet. I put one foot in slowly, then pull it out quickly and giggle, then put it back in slowly again. I bring my back foot forward and have both feet in the water and I look up toward dad with a big grin on my face. His face reciprocates my own and he takes another small step forward so I take a step forward.

We stop for a while and he points out the seagulls to me and tells me things about how the sun moves and where it's located in the sky and other things that I don't understand. I'm knee deep and he's ankle deep. He takes another step forward and I take another step forward. I'm waist deep and he's almost knee deep. He takes another step forward and his full weight drops, pulling him under the water and heaving me down with him. The undertow suddenly catches us both, turning us down and under the water. Churning and bubbles and all murky darkness.

This is where I died. I can say that. In Florida at age two I died, but a power far larger than Richard could ever imagine, shook the glass and saved me. My mom's words rang throughout my dad's head and he held on. I could feel my hand having the blood squeezed out of it. Down in the water and out to the sea, we somersaulted around and he could hear her words.

My dad regained his footing and we popped up together. He said I was laughing like I had just had the ride of my life. It was more that I now had a life to ride. Looking back on it now, I wonder if shaking the glass made someone else's egg die inside. I wonder who had to die so that I could live. I feel I'm on borrowed time.

***

I died again at eight-years-old. I had this child sitter who sometimes watched out for me if my mother couldn't whose name was Cathleen. I would go to her house with her three kids and it was usually a lot of fun. On this particular morning, while I was packing to go over to their house, mom squatted down to my level and grabbed both of my shoulders real tight. I thought she had found out I had taken some chocolate out of her secret stash.

"Drewster, I need you to listen to me real carefully now, okay? You listening."

I nod my head.

"You absolutely, under no circumstances, are allowed to swim today. You got it?"

I look at her strangely.

"If someone asks you to go swimming, you say no, okay? And I don't want you to try to save anyone's life. I know you and I know you'd go in after someone if they were in trouble and you need to promise me that today you won't do that. Do you understand what I'm saying?"

I nod my head.

"You know that mommy sometimes sees things that other people don't see, right? And you need to trust me today, got it?"

I nod my head.

"Say okay?"

"Okay."

"Okay, sweety. Take care of yourself." She kisses me on the forehead. "Now go get ready."

I run away, a little confused, but the rules are simple. Today I can't swim.

The phone conversation with Cathleen goes a little differently.

"I know you don't believe me, but that's what's going to happen."

"Mrs. Linscott, we're not going anywhere near water today. Nowhere. It can't happen. All we're doing is stopping by my Aunt's house quickly and they don't have a pool and then we're going to the discovery zone. We're going nowhere near water."

"You need to tell Mark-."

"I'm not telling my son anything. And it's not going to happen."

"Cathleen, I know what I saw and Mark is going to talk one of you're daughters into jumping in the water and she can't handle the current. Drew jumps in after her and they both end up drowning."

"Mrs. Linscott, you can't possibly ask me to believe such an absurd –"

"—Listen to me very carefully Cathleen. People have been telling me my entire life that I'm off my rocker; they've told me I'm crazy; they've told me I deserve to be locked away; they've told me I'm over reacting. Well let me tell you something, I don't give a shit about what you *think*. I'm telling you what's going to *happen* and if you don't go by any water today and this all just blows over then I'll be the happier for it, but if I'm right and something does happen than you better have a damn good lawyer because I'm going to make sure both you and your son –"

"Me and my son, what? Mrs, Linscott, I'm watching after your child in case you don't remember and this is a favor for you and your threatening me?" Cathleen was one of the few people who was as tough as my mother and she knew how to handle her. I think it's why they got along so well.

"Trust me, if I could watch after him today, I would, but I can't miss this meeting and I need to be able to trust you. If you don't think you can do it though, I'd rather take the risk of leaving him home."

"Nothing is going to happen. I'm telling you, we're going nowhere near water."

Nothing ever happens the way you expect it. People drive all the time, speeding at ninety or a hundred miles per hour, and nothing ever happens to them. They say they're fine, that they can handle it. You never expect it when there's a wet leaf patch in the middle of the road or a deer jumps in front of your car or some kid decides to take his or her bike across the highway. You can do something a million times and everything is just fine, but all it takes is for one thing to not go as planned and your whole life can change in an instant. One instant is all it takes. Dinosaur to cat. One instant.

That day in Florida, my dad never expected there to be a drop in the sand. Somehow a giant shelf was created by the tide a small distance away from the shore. The drop caused him to lose his balance and fall. The undertow happened to be there at that exact second. Sometimes the planets really are all aligned and sometimes they're not, but all it takes is that one time. It is one thing to be caught off guard, but it's quite another if even after that speed limit sign passes you by, you're still going ninety.

I watched out the entire day for water. We were at Cathleen's aunt's house for more than a little while. The whole time I kept looking out for a pool, or a pond… anything. I kept eyeing over to the neighbor's house, and through the back yard, looking for a small patch of blue or mossy green to stay away from. On the drive to the discovery zone, I looked out for nearby streams even as we sped by them at ninety miles per hour— we were running late.

By the time we got there, I had given up looking. It was only a small strip mall with a discovery zone in the middle. We walked inside and as she was buying the tickets, I saw her stars suddenly line up. Her eyes became wide and her hand sped to the outside of her jeans pocket. She patted it twice before reaching her hand inside.

"Shit. Kids come with me." We walk back to the car and she looks into the window. "Shiiiiit." The keys are lying on the front seat and the car is locked. She turns to all of us. "Stay right here, I'm going to go inside and make a phone call. Nobody move." She walks away and when she's out of earshot, Mark starts whispering to us.

"You guys want to go swimming?"

Huh? I immediately ask in my head.

"Why would we want to go swimming, *mor-on*? We don't even have bathing suits," says Beth, Mark's younger sister with a snobbish adolescent tone.

"We can go in our clothes, *dum-my*. Why you have to be such a spoil sport. I bet you don't even have the guts to jump in with your clothes on."

"Do to, I just don't feel like it."

"I'll bet you your Dolly doll, you won't."

"You have my Dolly! I hate you Mark! I knew you took it. I just knew it."

I must be blind, because I have no idea what they're talking about. Swimming? Where? Was there a place in the discovery zone? I start looking around again and it doesn't take me long to find it, but when I do, I feel like a load of bricks fall into the pit of my stomach. I am a cartoon character who has walked off the edge of a cliff and is still floating in the air waiting for the inevitable. A muddy looking river is flowing behind the strip mall, but one could only see it if they were looking closely in between it and an office building a few meters away.

"If you jump in first, I'll give you your stupid doll back."

When Mark reaches the end of this sentence, we watch as Cathleen's head suddenly whips toward the water. Then back at us. Michael and Beth are already in the middle of taking their shoes off, but they look up to catch Cathleen running back at us like a charging bull that has been tormented. We're all in red with shock because Michael can't figure out how she heard us. She stops an inch away.

"If any one of you dares go in that water, I will make sure you don't have a drop of fun for the rest of your natural lives. No desserts, no video games, no television, not even pizza. I'll have you sitting in your rooms with nothing but a book till you're eighteen. Mark, if you put a finger in that water, I swear I'll chop it right off and if you dare talk one of them into going in I'll make sure your father beats the living hell out of you. DO NOT GO IN THAT WATER." She turns around and starts the walk back toward the Discovery Zone.

We all stand still for a minute in complete awe of her divine motherly senses.

"Could she hear us?" Mark whispers.

At age two I died and at age eight, I died again. It's amazing how afraid of death we all are when we've all died so many times. The point is in the end, it only matters who is truly shaking the glass and I'm aware now of how powerless the Richards and Josephs really are.

Mom made countless predictions. She woke up one morning and turned to dad, "Oh my God. The shuttle is going to explode."

"What? What shuttle?"

"The space shuttle. The Challenger."

Two weeks later it did.

Another morning my mother told my dad that he would be sent on an errand to a certain location. She said he would be going to a place with a large open field and an old industry building.

"Now listen carefully," she said to him, "you're going to be looking for the entrance and it's going to be down a small dirt pathway a few feet further down from when your partner asks where it is. You won't be able to see it right away, but you will. Now, after you get down that pathway you're going to come to a swinging red door. Open it and you'll find a cement block that you can use to prop the door. It will still be too dark in there to see, but trust me, walk straight back from where the first door is and head right through the dark and you'll get to a second door. Open that, and there will be a second cement block just like the first that you can use to prop the door."

My dad went to work that day and the first thing that happened was he was given an assignment to scope out an old warehouse for extra wires. His partner and him arrived on the scene and it was exactly how my mother had described it to him.

"Where do you think the entrance is?"

Dad looked at his partner and smirked. "Watch this." Dad walked down the dirt path, opened the door, and propped it.

"How did you, wait...where are you going?" Dad walked off into the darkness. His partner watched until a few seconds later he heard the sound of shifting metal, then watched as the door opened. Dad propped it, and his partner walked over to him.

"You been here before?"

"No," he says with a laugh, "but my wife was last night."

Another time, mom and dad were sitting in an airport waiting for their flight, when my dad turned to my mother, "I have a bad feeling about the flight. Can you make sure it's going to be okay?"

Mom closes her eyes for a minute, then opens them.

"Yeah, everything's going to be fine. A woman is going to become claustrophobic and need to be carried off the plane and the flight's going to be delayed twenty minutes because they'll have to find her luggage, but the flight will be fine."

"Okay, good."

Once on the plane, my dad was seated next to another woman instead of my mom and my mom was placed behind him. A few minutes later, the flight assistants are seen helping someone off the flight.

"Oh my Gosh, I hope she's okay," says the woman next to my father.

Dad laughs, "Yeah, she's fine. She was a little claustrophobic, but the flight's going to be delayed another twenty minutes because they have to get her luggage off the plane."

The woman furrows her eyebrows and looks upon my father speculatively. Then the loud speaker comes on.

"I'm sorry ladies and gentleman for the disturbance, but the lady who was carried off the flight is going to be fine, she was having a small case of claustrophobia. We are sorry to tell you though, that the luggage carriers will need to find her luggage so we will be hanging out here for another twenty minutes. We're sorry for the delay and we'll let you know as soon as we're ready for take off."

The woman turned to my father with horror in her face, "How...how...how did you know that. Are you on the flight staff?"

"Nah," my dad laughed. "My wife told me."

My father was adopted. When he was in his mid thirties he became determined to find his birth mother. He had hired a private detective to see if he could find her, but he found out very little. Only a potential name and where she used to come from up in Maine. Dad was ready to give up, when mom stepped in.

"I'm beginning to think I'll never find her," Dad says discouraged.

Mom groans "Fine, I'll help you." She gets up and goes to one of the drawers in the kitchen like she's performing an agonizing chore. She opens it and pulls out the phone book. She brings it back to the table, opens it up, sifts through the pages and then points to a name.

"There. Nancy Bess Thorn. That's your mother."

Dad looks up to her with utter disbelief, but the last name fit. He looks at the name over and over again, next to the twelve other Thorns listed.

The private detective had traced her to Maine and Massachusetts, but he had never thought to look in New York. Dad couldn't comprehend it. Could it really be true that someone he'd been missing his entire life was really only a twenty-minute drive away? Mom gets up, grabs the receiver, and hands it to him.

"Here," she says. Dad sits paralyzed in shock. Mom goes back to the phone with the phone book and dials the number.

A soft spoken woman answers, "Hello?"

"Hello."

There's a long pause, "Yes?"

Dad struggles with the words he wants, "Is your name Nancy Thorn?"

"Why, yes, this is she."

"Is this Nancy Thorn from Northern Maine?"

Nancy laughs to herself, "Why yes it is. May I ask who this is?"

Dad continues questioning, barely able to comprehend the conversation. His hand holding the receiver shakes, "Did you ever happen to give up a child for adoption?"

There's another long silence.

"Why yes, I did. That was a long time ago. May I ask who this is?"

"Well, I believe this is that child."

A beat. "Is this William Linscott?"

Dad's mouth opens wide and he falls back into his chair. "Yes," he starts off, "yes, how did you know?"

Nancy laughs on the other end of the line, "I cheated," she said, "I looked at the name of who you were being adopted to and the name they had given you."

Dad can't even breathe might as well speak.

Nancy continues, "I guess this means we should make a date. We have a lot of catching up to do."

"Yes" Dad says with tears streaming down his face, "yes we do." And dad was the happiest mom had seen in him in years.

Mom used to tell me my test scores before I even took the test. I hated it.

"Drew, did you study for that test."

"Yesss, mom."

"You sure you studied well enough."

"Yes, mom, now leave me alone."

"Sweety, I think you should study a bit more."

"No, mom. I told you I studied already, it's not going to be that hard of a test."

"Not that hard of a test, huh?"

"No...Wait, why?"

"Because you're going to get a 77."

"What! A 77. No, I'm not."

"Okay."

"You really think I'm going to get a 77?"

"Mhmm."

"Fine." I snorted back, "I'll study more."

I studied for another hour and a half for that test and when I got it back, the grade read 77. I didn't know what that meant.

Would I have gotten a worse grade if I hadn't studied more or would I have gotten the 77 no matter what or did I only get the grade because my mom said I would? I didn't like it and she kept doing it till I yelled at her to stop. All I knew was that it pissed me off and I didn't want to hear about anything. I figured knowing might disturb the original outcome I may have been destined to and I didn't know if it would affect it in a good or bad way.

I tell Jessica all this and she sits back tentatively and listens.

"There's one more thing." Jessica's eyes stare at me reflectively, trying their best to show as little emotion as possible. "My mother has a friend who's also a sensitive. When I was twelve we visited her house and at one point she pulled me aside and told me that mom was going to get very sick, but she told me that I was the only one who could save her."

"And what do you think that means?"

"I guess that I'm the only one who can save her life, but I don't know how." Jessica's silent and Jessica's never *this* silent. Normally she'll have a question posed or she'll try to get to the heart of what I'm saying, but I don't think she's interested in any of that right now. Her head is tilted down and her eyes are unmoving. I don't know if I've hit her with too much. I don't know how she's supposed to take what I can't even make sense out of and I've been dealing with it for a lifetime.

"I've arranged for you to speak with the dean," she finally says after a long minute, "so that you can get those two weeks off. I don't think it should be a problem. He'll send a notice to all your teachers and you'll be given the work to make up."

"I think this is it."

"What's it?"

"My chance to save her."

"You seeing her?"

"It makes sense. Something's going to happen and I need to be there."

"What makes you so sure?"

"What else could it be? I have to do this. I have to go see her."

"You think by you being there it will somehow prevent your mother's death?"

"I don't know, but it seems to fit. Maybe preventing her suicide or I'll be there when she has an emergency. I don't know, it just fits. I *feel* it. I have to go, thank you, Jessica."

I go to see the Dean, but I have to go through his assistant first who tells me that I won't get two weeks off. I tell her that I already cleared it with all of my professors and that they were fine with it. She says that she doesn't believe me and goes into talking about her aunt having cancer and that she knows how I feel. I have the sudden urge to kick her in the ovaries.

She goes on to tell me what type of cancer her aunt had and that she was sick for six months before she died. She tells me all of this without me barely saying a word like I'm her therapist. This is the woman who has the next door neighbor who is an axe murderer and one day she shows up on the news saying, "I had no idea Karl would ever do something like that. He always seemed like the nicest guy." My mom's had cancer for six years, not six months, but I don't say anything and I don't want to be thrown into a cancer competition. "No, my situation is worse than yours."

"No, mine is."

It sounds like Richard and Joseph fighting over the egg except this is people dying. It's not good, none of it is, and everyone handles things differently. Nobody's experience is exactly the same as anyone else's. Some people have brothers and sisters, I don't. Some people are older and some people are even younger. This woman was thirty-five. Some people have a father who can seek help from his friends. My dad doesn't have any real guy friends. Some people are closer to their sick loved ones than others. I hate my mom and I love her to death as it usually goes with people whom you are so similar to. She can make me mad as hell and she can make me want to hold her for hours when she's upset. "I know how you feel." No, no you fucking do not. You may be able to relate, but you probably can't even feel the evil eye I'm giving you right now because you've turned the situation onto yourself like everyone else. I tell her "I'm sorry" about her loss and that's what people should stick to when they don't give a shit and they don't know what to say. Say "I'm sorry" and I'll be okay with that. Be fake to me now and I'll kick you in the ovaries until you develop a tumor. Then let's talk and I guarantee you'll have more patience than you ever had in your entire life. Looking death in the face, you may even find yourself able to listen for the first time and you start realizing all that you've missed out on by only really hearing yourself.

The dean ends up being nice and real. He's giving me the two weeks and even says he's going to put me in his prayers at night and nobody's ever said anything nicer to me in my whole goddamn life and it makes me want to break down and bawl my eyes out right there in his office. I say, "Thank you" and I mean so much more. These real people who come through at these times in your life, you never forget them. They're edged in an eternal file deep inside your heart where you think of them everyday of your life and hope that God shows mercy on them and their children and their children's children and that none of them will ever ever ever ever get as sick as my mom because they don't deserve it. Yet, I know they'll get it. Billy Joel said it, and now I'm saying it, "Only the good die young," and for some reason, God sure doesn't like his angels to be away from him for too long. Not that I blame him, I kind of want her back myself and she's not even out the door.

CHAPTER SIXTEEN

I'm in a hospital with bugs scaling up and down brown tiled walls. They eat away at everything and keep trying to get under my skin. Spiders, beetles, moths, centipedes, ants, flies, and they're all over.

My mom is lying down motionless, propped up on a stretcher bed like the one's you see going into the ambulance. She's got wires and cords all over her stuck in a million different places and there are doctors and nurse's crowded around her trying to help, but there's too much. They're fighting with one another as I sit on the floor with my head bent down in between my knees doing nothing at all. Helpless.

I try to look up, but I can't, so I allow my outer body self to watch from the corner of the room instead, which it does. I see my back resting on the wall. I watch as the doctors frantically move around her like dozens of hungry birds who have been thrown a handful of seeds. They're arguing about whether or not to move her when one of their arms gets caught in a cord in the chaos of the moment. The doctor turns and accidentally rips it out of my mother's arm and I hear the nurse's scream as blood violently sprays out and onto all of their clean white suits. Mom's body is eerily still, like she's already dead and her peridot eyes are open and gaze upwards, watching the sky and I can't tell whether they are empty or finally just know where to go.

The blood continues to squirt out in all directions and her body begins deflating as the liquid dumps out of her like a balloon that's been popped. She's withering down to nothing. Down, down, down, until she's flat on the ground, her skin like a pancake on that bed with only those eyes still popping up.

The doctors and nurses have all collided into one another while screaming their heads off as they run out. Everyone's gone except for me and her. It's completely silent except for the small reoccurring beep of the IV unit every four seconds or so. I get up calmly, walk over, and take her hand in mine, but it turns to ash almost immediately followed by the rest of her body. She sinks into the gurney and grass starts growing in all around her, so I stand up and walk away.

I walk up some stairs and into a large hallway that looks like it could be the waiting room to the hospital. There are two girls there that I know and they're both lying face down on beach towels. They stand up when I walk in and start talking to me, then suddenly they're caressing me, then they take their clothes off and I fall into one of them, but the fall jumps me into another hallway, this one much darker. I have a sawed off shotgun in my hand and somehow I manage to turn it around and point it at my head. I pull the trigger, BANG. Nothing happens, so I pull it again. BANG. Still nothing.

I'm still alive. BANG, BANG, BANG. Why won't I fucking die. BANG BANG BANG.

I hear laughing.

I give up on trying to kill myself and put the shotgun down and walk around a corner to see a class of young children with their teacher lecturing to them. When he sees me, he walks over and shakes my hand and tells me to wait where I am. The class of young kids stands up and follows the teacher around another corner where they wait behind a thick layer of glass. The teacher gives me the thumbs up signal and I look at him all confused because I have no idea what is going on. He then turns his head and I see him push a button. I hear the sound of a monkey in pain doing the "ooo, ooo, ooo" thing. I look forward to where the teacher is looking and there is a large gorilla there jumping up and down, getting an electric shock every time the teacher pushes the button.

The room is filled with dark blue and grey pillars. The floor is like a pile of ash except it is tiled like the walls in the hospital. "Ooo, oo, o" the gorilla jumps up and down with each buzz, getting more and more infuriated. The class is laughing and they laugh more each time the gorilla is shocked. The gorilla starts stomping and howling and the class keeps laughing. "Ooo, Ahhhhhh, Ooo, Ahhhhhh" the yelling gets to a higher and higher pitch. "Ooo, AHH AHH AHH, Ooo AHH AHH, Ooo AHH AHH AHH!" Buzz, Buzz, Buzz. Finally the gorilla starts banging on the floor and is about to jump right through the glass and rip the heads off of the teacher and each little kid and remove the smiles right off their pretty little bodies when suddenly from behind the pillars a purple train comes through and runs the Gorilla right over. I can hear the wooooosh of the train as it goes by at high speeds and then fade off into the distance. I walk over to where the gorilla was hit and I find that it was never really a gorilla at all, but a person in a Gorilla suit. Their body is splattered all over the floor in different areas, but not like you would think, instead the parts are embedded two-dimensionally within the tile, not lying on top of it. There is no blood. Each part is a two-dimensional mural plastered and cartoon-like on the tile floor. The entire face though happens to be in one square area completely squashed up against the surface facing me and through all the missing parts and through all the disjointed pieces to the puzzle, I can make out the face as my own staring right back up at me.

A voice tells me to wake up, so I do.

My mom's dying, I'm wearing a gorilla costume, my teachers and peers are laughing at me while they discharge tiny electric shocks of increasing strength into me and they watch as I squirm and scream until I can't take it anymore. Then they decide to run me over with a purple train and watch as my body paints itself all over the place because it doesn't know what's going on and for some reason, through all of this, I'm the only one who seems to think I'm going insane.

I wake up and brush the sweat off my forehead. I check my arms for holes in them for I've sworn the bugs have been living under my skin, but it seems fine. There's not even a mark. I'm getting ready to leave the real fake world and I'm feeling more relief than anxiety. I know once I get there everything will be better. The worst part is trying to explain real world things to the real fake world people. They ask, but I know they don't really want to hear about it. Most of them want gossip. I tell my closest friends that I'm leaving for a couple of weeks, but that's it and they know the deal anyway. Connor for the most part has fallen out of my life as expected. He doesn't talk to me and he doesn't feel the need to. His new wife, Michelle, has him locked in the dungeon under lock and key and I'm discovering how Michelle is a control freak, which is probably good for him anyway. He likes to be controlled and she's a control freak, they're perfect for one another. He's not even allowed to talk to Dori who had still remained close friends with him after they broke up, but now she's very upset by the whole thing. I felt this coming though.

It all happened after our training trip. That was the end of the line for me. With no true friends, no swimming, no girl friends, I've detached myself. I am a purple train off the tracks. I'm a crazy gorilla.

I cut the real fake world off because I couldn't deal with it any longer and since then my life has been a spiral of a world unknown, uncharted, and with no rules. A world where I can say the two letter word 'no'.

I first noticed how Connor was taking to one of the younger guy members of the team and befriending him, which was fine, but I knew he was doing it to distance himself from me. Like after a bad break up, you start hanging out with other people, but there's no reasoning for this other than that he knows I'm thinking of quitting the team. We have a long talk about it, which at the end he still doesn't understand why I want to quit. He blames me, especially because I was the one who got him into swimming and training hard. Things change, though.

"It's not about that, it's that my mind isn't with it anymore and with, you know...mom on my mind and everything, it's hard." I try explaining.

"I think you're psyching yourself out." He says blankly and with a shrug. It's like he's a different person. Or maybe I'm different.

"How so?"

"What's happening right now is one thing, but swimming is a part of you."

"Just because I'm not on the team doesn't mean I can't swim."

"I don't know, I don't see how you can abandon this. Abandon me like this."

"Abandon you? Dude, I'm right here. What? Because I'm not on the team doesn't mean we can't stay friends?"

"It'll change things."

"Now whose psyching themselves out. Connor, you need to understand where my head's at right now and let me figure this out. Nothing is dead set yet and I don't think there is any reason for our friendship to change because I'm not on the team."

"I don't think so, but whatever. You do what you want." He gets up and leaves to hang out with the younger boy and Michelle. I've been replaced. In the real fake world everything is replaceable. I thought I finally had a real friend. He hasn't talked to me since and I was relying on him to give me a ride home, which I soon figured out wasn't going to happen.

I call Dori who is luckily able to meet me at the airport and give me a ride. Out of nowhere she takes a seat next to me on the plane, you know, the plane that is going down at a goddamn angle. She straps herself in, closes her eyes real tight, and commits herself to going the rest of the way down with me. "I tell her she doesn't have to do this."

She says, "Of course I do. What else are friends for?" In one moment, I take back anything mean I ever said about this girl even in anger or as a joke. I take it all back and realize my instincts were right about her from the beginning. I have green eyes and Dori has blue. She becomes the person I can talk to about anything and she can tell anything to me. A beautiful girl with more guts than most guys is hard to find. She has blue eyes that can take darkness. I guess there's an exception to everything.

I walk into my home back in New York, but I don't recognize it from the inside. The kitchen and dining room table, which was once stacked with papers and bills is completely void of them. The DVD's and videotapes are nicely stacked in a new cupboard that is designed for that purpose, so that each title is facing outward. I give it a little spin. It twirls around, with each side containing more tapes. I feel a choke in my throat as a tear comes to my eyes, which I hold back with all my might. I go up to my room where all the child like stuff has been painted over with a new white wall and there's a cool looking rug on the floor next to my bed. Mom used to yell at me for throwing my wet towels on the bed after a shower. I told her I didn't have a place to hang them and they always fell off the doorknob. Now, I look at the back of the door and there's a steel rack with hangers attached to it.

For years I screamed back at her about things. I called her a hypocrite when she told me to clean my room. I told her she was a bitch for making me keep all my stuff and not letting me throw anything away. She would tell me I'd grow into it or you'll want this someday or this is too nice you can't throw it away, but everything's changed. Everything I ever yelled at her about since as far back as I can remember is now the way I told her it should have been. She threw out the old stuff, and cleaned it all, shaped it, sculpted it into something I had always envisioned. She changed everything for me. There's no way I could argue with her. There's no way I could put up a fight and throw something back in her face no matter how much I wanted to. If you could step back and really imagine all the shallow problems you've ever had with either your parents or your children, or your spouse, and really look at them for what they are, and make the conscious choice to change for them and become a role model for them or give in to their fun and their choices. Could you imagine quitting smoking or stopping drinking? Could you imagine finally letting go of their baby blanket or encouraging their dreams on every step of the way? Give it all up for someone else—that's what she did. She gave up all her bad habits to make me happy.

I ask dad if she did this and he gives a solemn nod. I'm speechless. I ask him how long it's been like this and he says a few months.

"And she's kept it like this?"

"Mhmm."

"Why? Why did she do all of this?" I know the answer, but I want to hear it.

"Because she loves you, Drew. She's always loved you, and I guess she realized what all this was."

"What was it?"

He looks me dead in the eyes. "Junk. Pure junk. It's all it ever was. What's important is what you remember and she's losing that."

We go to the hospital and even on my anti-anxiety medication I can still feel my insides shaking uncontrollably, making their way outward to my hands and legs. My brain's even beginning to rattle. Stepping onto the elevator, I realize I haven't been on one of these in a long time. The doors close and the elevator moves quickly upward and I know this is a good hospital. You can tell how good any hospital is, not by the way it looks, but by how fast the elevators move. I visited my Grandmother in hospitals and my mother in hospitals all over New York and I'll tell you that a slow elevator can be what kills you.

This one hospital in the Bronx took twenty minutes for the elevator to arrive. I watched my Grandmother in the stretcher, in pain, waiting there in line with all the others. Moaning and moaning, and I say to mom as a joke, "I hope they at least have the ER on the first floor." She turns to me and tells me that we're going to the ER.

"You're kidding me. What floor is it on?"

"The 17th."

"You're kidding me. Why would they do that?"

"I don't know, Drew."

"It just doesn't – "

"—Just be quiet, Drew. I'm stressed enough as it is."

So we waited and waited. I watched this one older woman with half her face burnt and one arm in a cast sit up and start screaming. The medical staff pushed her back down forcefully and held her there. I waited for a needle, a sedative, anything, but it never came. I realized the only thing worse than having to go to this hospital would be having to work in it. I think I'd rather be dead then listen to people die everyday waiting for a goddamn elevator.

"Why are we here?"

"Because they have very well-trained doctors."

"Let me guess, they keep them on the 18th floor?"

Her head snaps in my direction and her face expresses a lividness that should remain forever untested which tells me to both stop being a smart ass and to shut the hell up so I swallow hard and do exactly that.

There's something about the elevator. I guess we're all either going up or down. Either way, it's best if we get there as fast as possible. What's the point of having a good doctor if you can't even make it to him or her in time? If you ever have a loved one who becomes extremely ill and you wait longer than three minutes for that elevator, I'm telling you right now, get the hell out of there.

The elevator moves fast to the seventh floor and even through the shaking, I'm relieved to know she's being taken care of. The doors open. The air in the hallway is thick as molasses and it feels like it takes hours to get to her room. It's like my eyes aren't my own. I'm looking through the lens of a camera, more documenting than actually feeling and experiencing. The walls are white with pictures of people in abstract landscapes, and they're all alone.

I hear tiny beeps from life support units, heart monitors, and I.V.'s making their way up and down the hallway. It's like a dream, but the one difference is the smell. In any dream, you can know that you're dreaming because you'll never have that true smell that pierces through your nostrils and into the cavities of your brain and sticks there like a mothball. You can't smell death in a dream. You can't smell the air as it rises up in fear of itself. Air turns to shit, to piss, to blood, to dried blood, to swollen skin, to rotting skin, to burnt skin, to dry hospital food, to bland teas and boxed orange juices, to fear, to worry, to tears, to death and more death and more death and I blame the whole goddamn thing on the smell. Those windows that are already behind layers of thick glass are locked shut because they know people will jump from 20 floors up to get themselves back into some fresh air. I breathe this all in, and it becomes me. It lives in me, like mold on bread, once it's infected it will inevitably spread itself outward, it's just a matter of time till the smell gets me too. You can watch a billion different movies, read a trillion different books, go on a googolplex worth of adventures, but until you smell it all, you've never actually been on any of them. These poor people all have to waiver in their own stench. They say that the reason they keep the hospitals cold is to kill the germs, but anyone who knows anything knows that you mostly get sick from the cold. Cold *prevents* germs from spreading quickly and it stops the smell from crawling its way into every knick and corner of the hospital till the staff would run out screaming. You ever put your bread in the refrigerator to keep it from going bad? Well, that's what they do with your loved ones. They're refrigerating them, trying to preserve them as long as possible, till it's time for them to become compost.

I follow dad into the room. She's lying down, wires everywhere, eyes straight up, and for a second I think I'm back in the dream. I have an ocean swirling around in my head, but you know, you're supposed to be a man. You know, have some balls and all that crap. People die, people want to kill themselves, people get sick and it's all a part of the life you have to live. As long as you don't give into any of the sensitive shit, you're fine, right? RIGHT?!

"Hi." Mom's head turns to me with a smile so big it makes her eyes close a little.

It's like in an insane asylum when the guy goes completely crazy. He's hitting all the guards, muscles popping out of every orphic, veins like rivers on a topographical map, like he's hyped up on half a pound of PCP ready to jump out of his very skin, ready to kill everything and everyone...and then she says hi. I feel my muscles soften up. I pick my head up and look into her eyes and see that she's alive and that she can still smile. I guess everything really is alright.

"Hi, mom," I smile back at her. I lean over and hug her as best as I can without hurting her. I feel her kiss my cheek and I fight back that tear again. "How you feeling?"

"Ha," she says, "I think I've been better."

"Once upon a time, right?"

"Yeah," she turns her head to the window, trying to remember that time. "It seems like a long time ago."

I try to remember myself, but I can't come up with anything so I just nod my head and take hold of her hand.

Dad speaks, "Any news yet?"

"Yes, I think we can do it. Whether I want to or not, is another question," says mom, looking down into her lap.

"Why wouldn't you want to?"

Mom, takes another look at me and smiles again, "Have a seat, sweety," she says.

"Answer me! Why wouldn't you want to? This is the greatest opportunity we've had yet and you don't want to do it?"

I sit.

"Can you lower your voice?"

"Yes," he lowers his voice, but the strength of it is still there, "but tell me why?"

Even now that I'm here, I still don't know what the fuck is going on. "What's going on?"

Dad looks at me, then back to mom, "You going to tell him or should I not even bother bringing it up again?"

There's a knock at the already open door and a high pitched drawn out voice speaks, "Hiiii Honeyyy." It's my mother's friend Lena. She's an older woman, short, with curly red hair down to the top of her neck, and tight sun-leathered skin. Her presence brightens up the room. She's always smiling, and it forces us to smile too. Her black blouse and multi-colored skirt look funky together. My dad and my nickname for her is Mrs.McGoo, because we're pretty sure she doesn't even know where she is half the time. She's like the non-fake version of Kat, because she means well, does well for others, and knows a side of life that most would run off crying from and never come back. She would jump on the plane with me with a large grin on her face, cocktail in hand, and not even buckle in her seat belt. "They got any hot captains up here?" She'd say while looking up the isle. "No? I guess I'll just have to do with you, handsome." She reminds me of my grandmother.

"You look wonnnderful sweetheart." Every sentence of hers has an exaggeration to it like she's performing. She bends down and gives my mother a kiss. "And look at youuu!" She turns to me with open arms. She gets everyone outside their funk. All I wanted to do was be small and disappear and she reminds me of being larger than life and embracing everything. I force a smile.

"Hi Lena."

"Oh my God, he's so handsome. What are they feeding you at that school of yours, I'm going to get some for my husband." She gives me a wink and turns to my dad. "What's he all grim about?" Dad's still upset with mom and he's sitting propped up with his arms crossed.

Mom responds. "We were discussing the CyberKnife surgery."

"Ohhhhhh, So what's his deal?" She points at him secretively.

Lena looks at mom, I look at Dad, Dad looks at Mom, Mom looks out the window. Dad won't speak, I don't speak, Mom doesn't speak, Lena speaks. "Did I crash a party? What happened? Oh, honey, I got you this magazine," she jumps into bed with mom like it's a teenage bunk bed and they're going to share gossip together. "Now, they got all this stuff specifically for cancer patients. Look, aroma therapy, massage's, acupuncture. They have these self help groups and community get togethers. Oooooo, look it here, they have a golf course." She smacks my mom on the arm, "We could go golfing together." She looks at mom lying there with her, barely able to move, and mom gives her a smirk because she knows she's messing with her. "No, golfing? Oh, alright, we'll hold off on the golfing, but they got a pool!"

Mom turns and looks at me.

"They have on call psychologists and psychiatrists. I wonder if we can sneak you some good drugs."

"What do you think, Drew?" Mom turns her head to me.

I laugh, "I think you'd be better off putting a gun to your head, but that's just me."

"I think I agree with you," says mom, turning back to Lena.

"Oh, well," Lena lowers her voice and places her head down. The wind being taken out of her sails, "It was a thought."

I know Lena means well and I feel bad at ruining her attempt to make my mother feel better. So I think about it. And on second thought, I don't think it sounds so bad. A community of dying people who get together once or twice a week where you can watch each other decline. Make friends with people who you know are probably going to die and watch as some of them go before you and others stay healthier while you get sicker. Be able to swim one day and watch someone's hair fall out into the water the next. Talk to a bunch of people about their feelings with their individual experience; listen to people who have it worse off than you do or better. Listen to the parents with seven children whose spouse is a drunk or hasn't had a job in years. Share the same ambulance with someone as you're whisked off to the hospital. No, I guess I had it right the first time. If you're going to admit to being dead, you might as well be dead already.

What if they took all that money they spent on all those luxuries, all the therapy and all the medicine, and they put it into a hospital where you could just die. Maybe you're still looking good and feeling well enough to walk in yourself. You know you're going to die and maybe you've simply had enough. You could even be really old, maybe lost everyone you've ever known and you don't want to be around anymore. Common sense 101. I haven't had the course yet, but I think it should be added to the curriculum.

You walk in and see a nice receptionist with a great big smile behind a desk. She hands you a few papers to fill out, then you sit in the waiting room till you're brought in to see a doctor. The doctor examines the papers you've given him or her, which has to do both with past medical history and your own personal statement, but it doesn't faze you one bit because after going to countless hospitals, doing this over and over again, you have it in the back of your mind that these will be the last papers you ever have to fill and this brings you a sigh of relief. The doctor gives you a full check up to make sure that you really are "good" to die, old enough, sick enough, mentally ill enough or whatever it may be. After your clearance to the pearly gates or to the depths of hell, this doctor gives you a series of choices of how you would like to die. A nice common sense gift you know? Maybe they'll even get you a relaxation therapist while they slide the needle into you. Whatever you'd like. An over dose of Demerol or

Dilaudid or Viagra even. Whatever makes you happy and they'll give you the largest dose they know will fully do the trick.

You're still semi-conditioned self drops down to the ground like a chopped elm tree. You got the biggest smile in the whole fucking world on and if someone asked you how you were doing and you could still talk for once you would say "good" and you'd mean it. Somehow, the world having enough logical sense for you to die happy when you knew your time was up, made you that much happier. Such common sense could only mean that there has to be a God somewhere because he let you go out with a bang and a half. Whatever family or loved one's you have will get to remember you with happy thoughts in mind and a visual of you that was still pleasing. I'm sure even the funeral home caretakers will breathe a sigh of relief as they can easily package your limp body into a beautiful showing that they can be proud of. If this place doesn't exist, your next best bet is to take all the money you would spend on these cancer communities and give it to someone with a future, someone who needs it, and use the rest to blow your brains out or whatever way you find best to end it all.

"We could buy you a really fast car?"

Mom laughs at me, because she knows where I'm going with this, "So I can drive it over a cliff?"

"Yeah. At least you'd go out with a bang, right?"

"Right." She says sullenly and turns back to Lena, reminding me that her life isn't a joke. I shut my mouth and become serious again. My last thought being, when God created the Universe did he imagine people gathering together to die in a death community?"

I have an assignment for a writing composition class, but I can't do it. You're supposed to write about something objectively, an object or place that you know a lot about. It's called classic prose. I don't really know a lot about anything, I just pretend like I do because I'm unsure what is actually true, especially if "they" you know, the hierarchs, tell me it is. I only know what people understand and what they don't. So everything I am is subjective, but it's subjective towards people and that makes me right about 65% percent of the time which again is still passing in the real fake world. I told you once that my dad says you can be right and still be wrong, well it works the other way around. *1984*'s War is peace and all that crap. What I'm getting at is I want to take all the hate in the world and make it good, I want to take all that's wrong in this world and make it right. I understand that this is different for everyone, but remember, we've all accepted it being lumped into two categories; what most of us feel is right is deemed right and what most of us feels is wrong, is considered wrong. This is where the 65% comes from.

Take a step back, turn around, get naked, stand on your head for two minutes, attempt peeing into a cup, cough, go see a doctor and tell him that there's something wrong. Your urine is going the wrong direction, your privates move when you cough because it's been so long since you've seen yourself that way and for some reason your thinking has become a hell of a lot clearer from all the blood that's just gone to your brain from standing on your head. On second thought, tell your doctor you know what's wrong. You thought you had cancer, but you've just never stepped out of your boundaries before. It's easy to have the two confused.

I'm stalling.

I want to find something that at least most of you will hopefully understand; things like pain, love, fear and death. I want to take all of those and show how they are all the same and they are all nothing. Pain is love, pain is fear, pain is death. Love is pain, love is fear, and love is death. Fear is pain, fear is love, and fear is death. Death is everything and it is nothing at all. I'm trying to show you what I need to show myself because when I look at her, all these things seem to lead to one straight road in which we all must take. She's going to die. I'm going to die. I'm going to turn into a helpless withered, skin wrinkled, bed pissing thing. When I look into her green eyes, I see everything that she did for me and I see nothing because I don't want to. I am numb. Jessica asks me if I've ever heard of the five stages of death. I smile and tell her that I'm not in denial, I'm accepting too much. There are things I don't remember that I wish I could. I decide to write about mom for my assignment.

Sharon Beaumont was raised in a small apartment in the Bronx of New York City. Her father woke up early every morning to avoid his wife, feed his birds, grab a cup of coffee and head out to the park to play chess for the rest of the afternoon. Her mother who spoke yidish, especially while making Sharon breakfast, was lively and full of energy. After sending Sharon off to school in the morning, she would head out to work at a local school, which was the only means for supporting the family. Sharon was weary to ask her mom for anything because she knew she couldn't afford it, but she knew that she'd give her anything to make her happy and that she would never say no. Because of this, Sharon kept a small jar in which she kept all her savings in the world propped on top of her dresser so that she could one day buy something special. One morning at twelve years old, she found the jar gone, and her only brother gone with it. He purchased a car and drove far away, for he had always complained about their lifestyle and no longer wanted any part of it. There was only a note, "I owe you." – Sharon cried for days.

Sharon's short height, pudgy figure, and curly hair were attributes inherited by her mother, but when she grew to be a teenager, she lost the weight and straightened her long black hair coming into her own. In school she was the minority and she spoke of the three tall black girls who would take her lunch everyday or beat her up trying. In reaction, she wised up and began packing only tuna fish sandwiches. The black girls took one look at it and screamed in disgust. Pushing Sharon down to the ground, they would throw her lunch back at her and walk away. After a few weeks, they stopped trying. Sharon said she did her best not to be racist, having many black friends throughout her lifetime, but the three black girls would always stay in her mind.

Besides witnessing common knife fights, Sharron would be walking down the hall and approach kids passed out on floors with drool hanging from the sides of their lips and needles still stuck in their arms. She would hug the walls, trying to get by them, because she knew how they would occasionally spring up and grab her. When this happened, she was always able to fight her way off, but she had a few close calls. This environment made her tough, smart and motivated her to escape. With receiving all A's and being pushed through all the accelerated classes, Sharon graduated high school at the age of sixteen.

She had been aware of her sensitive abilities since she was eight-years-old. Her first real encounter was when her mother called and before anything was said Sharon screamed over the telephone, "Daddy got into a car accident." Her father had received a broken leg from the accident and her mother would be late in picking her up from school. This did not come to a surprise to her mother because her father had the same gift, but he never spoke of it. He sometimes did things with no present reasoning to them, but which came forward seconds or minutes later. She would ask how he knew and he would say nothing or simply shrug his shoulders. Sharon's mother would constantly complain about it because she said with all his knowing he couldn't bet and win on one single damn horse no matter how many times he went to the tracks.

When Sharon saw her future husband for the first time, she hid. She was walking down the street on a usual day when she looked across the road and saw a man about six feet tall with broad shoulders, short black hair, and a long beard. A voice suddenly popped into her head, "You're going to marry that man." In fear she took the hat on her head and plunged it down over her eyes and walked in another direction. Her future husband William, later said that he probably would have never seen her if she hadn't done that. Sharon's voice said, "You're going to marry that man." William's voice said, "What a strange girl." They were both right.

A few weeks later, Sharon was surprised to see the man talking to her father in the park, just in passing. Her father didn't talk to anyone unless it involved betting or chess. Afraid again, she ducked her head down and scuttled with her short legs in another direction.

Sharon had attempted college, but with no knowledge of the possibility of scholarships, she went to the nearest and cheapest school, which she hated. After dropping out, she was desperate for a job, and decided to offer guitar lessons. A woman named Kerry called

Sharon up, had a short interview with her over the phone, and made an appointment. Midway through, sitting down with Kerry, guitars in hand, she heard the front door open and William walked in. She said she almost dropped the instrument right out of her hands. Finally having no place to hide, Sharon gave in and was receptive to talking with him.

Kerry was William's first wife. He claims he married her because he was young and I quote, "she was a sex machine." William, though, found himself having six-hour long conversations with Sharon sitting in a hallway together long after Kerry's guitar lessons were over. He said he was never able to talk to a woman for that long before. Nothing happened, though. They remained friends and luckily Kerry kept wanting guitar lessons up until she cheated on William. Apparently it had been going on for a while and everyone knew it except for William, especially one of his good friends who happened to be the culprit himself.

Losing everything so quickly, William was able to turn to his good friend Sharon, who although young, had the maturity of a thirty-year-old. Up till then, he hadn't seen Sharon as anything more than a beautiful friend, but with talking for longer and longer hours, he came to terms with how special she was and never wanted to let her go.

Sharon was nineteen when she got married, William was twenty-five. Sharon's first child was a miscarriage, and her second died at birth. Drew Linscott was conceived on William's birthday, it was Sharon's gift and at age thirty-three, she found herself with a baby boy. The boy was raised mostly by his father and baby sitters because Sharon was working full time and was attempting college again. It took seven years to receive her degree in business, but she achieved it at top of her class and Summa Cum Laude.

The boy turned out to be shy and quiet, but always had a smile on his face. Sharon and the boy watched rainstorms together. She taught him how to play board games and play cards. She let him win when he was really young and then how to deal with losing when he got older. She swam with him in the pool and always had a large towel to wrap him up in when he got out. The boy would always tell her how tall she was and she'd always tell him back that she was really very little. The boy would always reply, "But you're big to me mommy."

The boy drew pictures of her standing on top of the world, because she would always protect him and was the toughest person he knew. She taught him how to be kind to girls and always what to do. "Be spontaneous," she'd say. "Surprising a girl can really make them happy. If only your father would bring me home some flowers once and awhile." When Sharon wasn't looking, the boy then went to William and asked him to get mommy some flowers. William at first didn't understand where his son would come up with such an idea, but soon figured that his wife must have alluded to it somehow. The next day he came home with a large bouquet of purple flowers and Sharon looked at the boy and smiled knowing what he must have done.

She taught the boy how to do his own laundry after he asked how it worked.

"So do you know how to do it now?"

"Yeah, it seems easy enough."

"Good, then you can do it from now on."

"But-"

"Eh, eh. You're a big boy now, you need to know how to do your own laundry."

Sharon showed the boy how women need their own space, how to change the roll when it's empty, and how to put the seat back down when you are done using it. "When you have a home of your own someday," She said "you need to have at least two sinks or even better, if you can manage it, two bathrooms, oh, and a large mirror because ladies need their space in the mornings, you understand? We make a big stink about getting ourselves made up for the day and in that hour or even *two hour* period – yes it can take that long – men need to most importantly stay away and second to be very very very patient. Okay? After a woman gets all dressed up and has her make up done and everything, she's going to ask you how she looks, and you have one response ready and that's that she looks beautiful. You got that? Beautiful. Let me hear you say it."

"You look beautiful mommy."

"Good, you can't go wrong. Because even if a woman looks awful she's already put a lot of time into getting ready and to be perfectly honest with you, she probably doesn't even care what you think at that point. She's being rhetorical. Do you know what that means?"

The boy shook his head.

"It means she's really just talking to herself. If you would like to make suggestions that is acceptable, not preferred, but acceptable, but again it can only follow after what?"

"You look beautiful."

"That's right. Beautiful, and don't forget it. Your mommy knows she looks like a fat cow sometimes, but your dad always makes me feel good because whenever I ask him how I look, he always says I look beautiful and that makes me smile."

Sharon taught the boy how to read body language and how to speak without speaking.

"When you speak to someone you make eye contact with them. Most men have a terrible habit of not looking at you when you speak, especially in the working world and if you learn to look someone in the eye it shows trust and confidence. Women love confidence and they love it when you show them enough respect to look them in the eyes.

If you're having a conversation with someone and you notice they're looking off into another direction, or fidgeting, it probably means they don't want to talk to you anymore. Don't take it personally, it may just mean that they are busy and just have someplace to go, but other times they may not be interested in the conversation. If that happens, politely find an excuse to go or join another conversation. There are other signs of someone not wanting to talk, like if a person has their arms crossed like this."

She crosses her arms.

"It's called body language, Drew. If someone's leaning forward it shows interest. If they're leaning back it shows a lack of care. Watch out for it and you'll pick up on it more and more. It will help you to become aware of your own body language and what it shows to others."

When he was younger, Sharon took her son to swim practice on Saturday mornings. She would read to him to help him fall asleep. She helped him with his grammar for school. She'd allow him to come into her bed in the mornings and put his freezing cold feet on her.

When he was older, he became more into swimming and drove everywhere on his own. He didn't visit her too often when she was in the hospital because she told him not to, even though she wanted him to. They fought a lot about things because they had grown to become similar to one another: stubborn in the worst ways, angry towards one another, and more than anything, defensive.

Sharon knew all of this, though. She had planned it. Her life lessons, her pushing everything she knew about life onto the boy and her constant forcefulness in making him independent was all part of the knowledge that she would leave him at an early age. The boy felt this, although he had no idea where it came from. He felt strong anger from her mere presence with no concept of why.

Sharon knew what she had to do, but she couldn't conceive of its reaction. It was impossible for her actions to be without consequences and most of all, the effect it would have on her from loving the boy, to pushing him away as gradually as she could, yet, still wanting him to be her little boy. It could not be every way that she wanted it and the boy didn't understand why he could not be everything that she wanted and still be on his own.

Apart from her wedding ring, Sharon wore a gold rose around her neck, which was a symbol of her idol Saint Theresa. Theresa, she said, was a performer of small miracles, not large ones. She had visions as well and died at a young age from illness. Sharon performed many small miracles in her life and helped people on a daily basis even at the expense of losing time with her family; time that she knew did not exist forever. You can tell how amazing of a person Sharon is just by looking at her right now, sitting in a hospital bed, propped up, and smiling. A few minutes cannot pass without the door opening from a friendly visitor whom she has touched somehow so dearly in her life. She carries with her those strong eyes and fierce will to live even with the knowledge of what she knows is coming.

Yes, that's my classic prose for my mother. Those are my objective thoughts. And even with knowing all of that and understanding how truly sympathetic I should be, I still can't help but think it's all her fault that she's going to die.

CHAPTER SEVENTEEN

It's the test. She told me I would get a 77 on it, so I studied harder. I still got the 77. If I had not done the extra studying for it maybe I wouldn't have gotten the 77, maybe I would have done worse, or better. If mom knows she's going to die, maybe she's not trying to beat it, maybe she's trying to accept it, but in this case does getting the lower grade mean you get to live?

My hatred towards her tells me she's done this to herself. She knows she's going to die soon, she's known it for a while, and I think she's made herself sick. Now I know she's going to die and I hate myself for that. Now for once, I *feel* it. The dominoes are going to fall and I know exactly how they will land. They are set up and I'm still standing here at the first one, wondering whether or not any of us have the power to stop it from tipping over.

Six years went by with many surgeries and recurrences where the doctors said she might not live and I was never worried. Now, I know too and it makes me as guilty as she is. There has to be some way to beat this.

"Psychosomatic," Jessica calls my shoulder injury. "Your mind wants a way out so your body reacts." Can one really make themselves sick? And if they can, can they make themselves better too? And how does knowing someone will die from drowning differ from knowing someone will die of cancer?

We're all just waking moments in time until the next waking moment.

I keep telling everyone that it's okay, I'm crazy, I'm insane. I hear myself laugh maliciously. My friend Chris looks at me as if he's not sure whether or not I'm kidding.

"HAHAHAHA."

I spin around in circles, beer in hand. I'm on my anti-anxiety medication. The party is crazy, the dancing is wild, the music is blasting. I laugh again, trying to breathe it all in. The room is spinning and I feel my smile turn into Richard's smile. I feel my eyes turn into Richard's eyes, becoming glossy and light.

"You want to make out?" I say to the girl with a bitchy face and large breasts. She's quiet and boring. Everyone's so fucking boring and not alive. We need to wake the fuck up!

"No," she says, disgusted.

"You sure?" I smile, my Richard smile with one hand on the wall as I lean down closer to her.

"Yeah, I'm sure, get away from me!" She pushes me away and I laugh my Richard laugh.

I tell Jessica that my mom is cancer free. They, the doctors, told me so.

I inhale another beer. The room is spinning, music is blasting. Everyone is living like they have a million years left in them. They all want to fuck each other, to *feel* each other, but none of them have the guts and so instead they grind and twist and get just as close as they can to destroying the perfect fake suburban life image of themselves without actually doing it. I sit on another girls lap and say "Hi," and don't forget to smile.

Who the fuck are you? I hear her eyes say to myself. Well, who the fuck am I? They don't care who you are or anything, they care what you put up front. A good face and a natural charm. Nobody cares. We're all "good". Well I think we're all disgusting and stupid so why not finally give into it.

The girl smiles and says "Hi."

"How is that possible?" Jessica asks. I tell her that mom went through with the CyberKnife surgery. I convinced her to. It was a procedure that uses homing missile technology to eradicate inoperable tumors.

"She had ultrasounds and sonograms and x-rays and bone scans and I don't know what else the fuck you call it," I say to Jessica. "She had them all and they say she's cancer free."

After the mindless chit chat, I try moving in again with the new girl and she pushes me away, "I'm not that kind of girl." She gets up and walks away, and I fall deeper into the seat and laugh with half closed eyes. Romeo was drunk when he met Juliette. They were at a party when they looked upon each other and fell in love at first sight. I've fallen in love many times at first sight and they all came under the category of me being drunk off my ass.

Do you think a sober person climbs their sworn enemy's wall because they're in love after one night? No, it's called being drunk, stupid, and horny. The greatest love story of all time follows this idea. It's a way to break the ice, then you can get to know each other and see where it goes. Because remember, we don't give a shit, we're all just "good" and we don't know anything about one another, so what else are we supposed to do? "Wilt thou leave me so unsatisfied?" It only works if you're Romeo or Leonardo Di Caprio.

"What satisfaction canst thou have tonight?" A kiss is all I ask, an exchange of your true drunken love for mine. Just for tonight. Then you can fall out of the picture as quickly as young Rosalin. It's all the same shit, we just call it by different names.

Fuck you head. Stop this.

Shut up and give in.

No.

Hahahaha, it doesn't matter what you think.

"What's wrong?" Jessica says. "You should be happy, that's great news." I look down at the ground. The real world tells me differently.

"I can't get used to it, you know? It's like everything has been up and down for so long, now I'm supposed to act like everything is normal again. It's like I don't want to let myself get excited about it to be let back down again. The whole thing seems unreal, like nothing's changed." Nothing has changed in the real world. The domino is still set up to fall in its place. It's just been delayed. I can feel it getting ready to fall. And maybe for once the problem is I actually *want* it to fall. I want it to be over.

On the last day of visiting, we were in the house and I asked mom to come sit down next to me on my bed. I told her I had a lot to say to her because I didn't think I would ever see her again. She said she didn't think she would ever see me again either.

Even with her being cancer free. I told her I loved her and thanked her for everything. Mostly everything went unsaid and we wound up lying down looking at the ceiling for an hour saying nothing at all. I wanted to feel her presence close to me one last time. Awake. Alive. Alert. Whatever the fuck you want to call it. I wanted to remember.

She eventually got up and said, "Goodbye". I didn't say anything. I continued looking up at the ceiling wondering what that word really meant and hating her for not giving me the opportunity to stay…Tell me to stay.

I had asked both of them and told them I wanted to. They insisted that I continue school, but I told them I didn't think I could. In the end, I left it up to mom. I said I would leave the decision up to her and I wanted the complete honest answer. She told me that I should finish the semester and that we'd bring it up again then.

I see caskets.

The government alcohol program brings us to a funeral home. They show us silver expensive caskets with black lining, mahogany wood caskets with gold lining, oak caskets with silver lining, bronze caskets with bronze lining. They show us all the different types of felt they put inside: rich red with crosses, gold with white dots, chocolate, china white, ivory white...

I see puppeteers.

I see large hands controlling small wooden figures in the shapes of people moving them around whichever way they want to. I see them placing the toy puppets in something, smiles on their faces.

I see caskets.

I see mom.

I see the vacuum they're going to use to take out all her insides before displaying her.

They make us give a eulogy, our eulogy, although they don't say that. They say they can't say that. Some people stand up behind the podium crying, some fearful, others make jokes. I'm the joking kind, with a little bit of seriousness in between.

I see hospitals, lots of them, and this one. They bring us to a hospital. They repeat that we can never tell anyone about these things that they do. It's for our benefit or else we could go to prison (they show us that too). They show us sickly people and more pictures. They bring us to a room where they say a recently deceased person is inside. They say we have to go in or we don't pass the program. I see girls crying and boys laughing.

They line us up inside, cramming us in. The first thing you get is the smell.

The pungency of body decay, piss, the bleach permeating off the floors from when they last cleaned it and now our cramped in hot bodies one next to the other. The guy has tubes sticking out all over him and a BPM machine, which I'm surprised doesn't read zero. He must still be on life support. Maybe he's an organ donor. He doesn't look dead. His skin is a milky white with a large laceration on his shoulder and leg. It's beginning to turn black and blue, which is the only evidence that he is in fact dead. They have an oxygen mask on his face inflating air into his stomach. I can see it moving up and down. He looks no more than thirty-five.

After a couple of minutes they take us out. More girls are crying now. One of them runs to me and hides in my arms. I don't know why they are doing this to them. Have the men suffer, we're the assholes anyway. No matter how many mistakes or how nasty some girls can be, at the end of the day, they're still girls. We're programmed for this crap, they're not. I guess there are exceptions for everything, but the girls here are crying and scared, and that's all I

see. I'm as bad as the people showing us these things, or maybe I'm
not.

I hear laughter.

It's okay, I tell Chris, I'm crazy. Read Poe's *Tell Tale Heart*,
read *The Cat in The Staircase*, it's the one's who deny it that are really
crazy. Like AA's first step, you have to admit it. I'm laying down the
sword, admitting to being like everyone else. I'm crazy, and it's never
felt so good. I just want everyone else to announce that they're crazy
too and it would all be okay. Let's just dream together and die
together and it will all be okay.

Everything is an alcohol-induced dream. Everything is an
intoxicated state. I see her more now than when she's two feet away.
She's in my memories so clearly. I know everything: the smell of her
skin, how it feels when she embraces me, the sound of her voice. I
could reach out and touch it. There's no yelling in memories, only
smiles, and no smell.

I can touch her long black hair before it all fell out, I can hear
her strong soothing voice before chemo made it weak and tired. She
used to laugh, now only I can laugh.

"Hahahaha!" But Richard's laughing now. This girl I'm now
in love with sinks into my dreams, into memories. She comes back to
my place with me.

Jessica says she'd like me to see the psychiatrist again for more medication. I tell her the medication hasn't been working, I thought it was for awhile, but it's not. She says it takes some time to get into my system. She asks if I've been taking it correctly and I say no. She looks down at her notebook. The pen in between her two fingers taps on the paper showing her disappointment in me.

The psychiatrist tells me about anti-depressants. I can see in his dark silvery eyes that he's a pill popper. I wonder how much money he gets for each prescription he gives out. "Given what I know about your past history, I think it would be best for you," he says with those silver eyes that are cold and uncaring. His eyes seem to infect his whole body, giving his entire presence a stone color haze. He seems more lifeless than the dead body was.

"It decreases your sex drive, doesn't it?'

"It has been known to do that in a certain percentage of males, but it doesn't go for everyone."

65% is passing. "Forget it."

"You can't sleep, right?"

"Yeah."

"You're anxious all the time, and having terrible dreams at night. How are your grades?"

"Fantastic. They say I'm a nobel laureate in the making."

"Sarcasm, great," he does the looking down at the notebook thing. "Well, you have all the obvious signs of depression, it's up to you what you want to do about it."

"I don't think that medication will help me, it's like alcohol classes, they only work temporarily, maybe they'll work for that night, but soon enough people start drinking again. You're not fixing anything, you're burying it. You do the same thing with cancer, you don't fix the real problem, you just take out the tumor and hope the disease will magically go away. Drugs are for the weak minded, I can beat this, I just need something to happen."

"Like what?"

"I need my mom to get better or to not get better."

"You mean die?"

"I just can't deal with the in between anymore."

"Weak minded, huh? So why don't you stop the alcohol?"

"Because I don't want to."

"You realize that is a classic sign of depression and alcoholism."

"I've seen the alcoholics, and I know about all the blah blah blah about how it is a progressive disease, but I'm not one of them. I don't drink during the day and if I drink during the week it's only a drink. I know most adults who come home and have a drink after work. I binge drink on the weekend, but so does everyone in college. You think I'm going to keep that up once college is over?"

"Are you asking me?"

"No. I know you're right through all my own bull shit. It's definitely possible, but I can't see the future, so why don't you tell me how everything's going to play out since you seem to know?"

"I think you should take the medication."

Fuck you. Shove it up your ass. "I'll think about it," I tell him.

I run up and down my hometown street. I think I'm looking for something, but I don't know what, something that's missing. I chase after a dog, then the dog chases me. Evil people stand around at the end of the block talking to one another in whispers. They look at me from underneath their fedora hats, a dark silhouette hiding the specific features of their faces. I know they won't let me out. They are the guardians of what I can and cannot do.

I run back to the house to tell someone; anyone, but I don't think anyone's there. The garage won't open and it starts to rain. I run around back and grab a key I didn't know was there and open the garage. It's empty, with scattered dust and a few remaining rakes and shovels. The light is still on. Someone must have left it on.

I skip the first floor and arrive on the second. There's no furniture, no pictures, no anything, just an empty house with off-white walls. I walk around a corner and see a man at the front door with his back to me. His shadow is cast in jagged lines across the floor. The silence floods my ears like sinking under water. I feel something chewing on my arm. I hear machinery: clank, grind, clank.

I hear my heart beating louder.

I get closer. The man is so still. I hear someone in my voice say, "Dad?" The man turns around. It is my father, but with the face of a puppet like a wooden pinnochio. A toy. He laughs at me. His metallic jaw clamps up and down maniacally. The front door swings open and a conveyer belt drags him out toward the front porch. He just stands still – watching me. Allowing himself to be dragged away...

It's like that moment before the roller coaster goes over the edge. That slow crank of the conveyer. Each clank brings your heart closer to bursting. CLANK CLANK CLANK CLANK CLANK CLANK...And he's smiling. He's being dragged away and he's still smiling. A large mechanic arm, prehistoric in size and scope, and with the end like a lock wrench, grabs him as soon as he reaches the porch. It sweeps him behind the pane glass windows at the front of the house, lifts him up, and whisks him away as quietly as he appeared.

I hear rattling.

I look down to my right arm. There is a purple bug, shaped like a snake, chewing through it, going around and around, spiraling its way up. It's boring one hole after the next, disintegrating my arm into nothing.

I hear screaming. I'm screaming.

I fall back further and further away from the house. I feel the bug still biting even after I wake up.

I put my left hand to my arm, feeling up and down.

"Are you okay?" Says a girls voice.

"Huh?" I hear someone else say, a voice that must be my own.

"Are you okay?"

"No, but that's okay. I'm going back to sleep."

CHAPTER EIGHTEEN

I was out of love again by morning. True love sealed with a kiss till morning with a true goodbye sealed with a kiss. Spread this across a lifetime and it's almost the same thing, it all depends on your sense of time.

I have no idea what was a dream and what was real. Even after the girl walks out the door, I'm not sure if I'm still asleep. I feel like an idiot. Everything I said and did, I didn't mean any of it. I'm not like that.

Alcohol classes don't teach you these things, a conscience does. Common sense disease. They focus so much on hurting yourself, but when you drink, you don't give a shit about yourself. For me, I don't give a shit before I start drinking, but it's other people I care about. I'm selfish, and I care...I don't know how else to explain it. There's no common sense in it I guess, but it's not my fault – I haven't had that class yet.

I woke up and no one has accepted and no one thinks they are crazy. The world is exactly the same as I left it. We bank on the fact that when we're dead, we won't have to deal with it. In the world I see, there are no classes. When someone does something wrong, it's acknowledged by everyone. If you killed someone, nobody would do anything. You kill someone else, nobody would do anything. They would tell you that it was wrong if they knew who you were, but that would be it. You'd kill and you'd kill and you'd kill, do wrong after wrong after wrong, until there would be nothing left. Like a young boy after beating the crap out of something, post-orgasm, they would lay back, exhausted. Once it's all gone and out of their system, they'd be forced to reflect on everything that they did. They would have to put it all into perspective and know it all, *feel* it all. No matter how many years it would take with everyone letting you make your mistakes and eventually you would learn. You would apologize for all that you had done and to everyone you had ever hurt as I am apologizing now. This would be your life with no prisons or laws. This would be the life where people didn't fear death like it was an end. This is how I feel. It's a new day, and I don't plan on being like that ever again.

My head's still spinning, but I remember everything, just not together. What is real and what is not. I remain silent for the rest of the day, thinking about how I'm the biggest hypocrite on the planet, who hates hypocrisy.

Class isn't the same as it used to be. I don't hear things as well. I'm trying so hard to hold onto the information, but it slips right back out. Certain information doesn't seem to matter anymore. I can pay attention for only a second before my mind drifts off again. Everything has the words, "if you're dead" at the end of it. Why does physics matter if you're dead, why does math, why does the molecular structure of a specific element, why does the anatomy of a fish, why do I have to know the names of the presidents, or the members of Congress or state vs. federal laws? My mind is off somewhere else because it is attempting to latch onto something, specifically something valuable for when I'm dead, something I can say I know and will always know.

At one point in time, I thought there was only one way to swim. Strokes have designs to them and coaches implement these onto their swimmers. This is how you kick, this is how your arms move, now practice. Do it again, do it again, do it again.

You get to a certain level from all your practicing that is fairly competitive, but then you taper off. You can practice all you'd like and you won't get any faster. After this point, you begin looking for advantages elsewhere by studying the people that are better than yourself. Well, that person is the fastest so their style stroke must be the best. You do what you can to mimic their stroke and you get faster, but not by much. You look at others who are good and attempt to combine the best attributes of each swimmer and make the perfect stroke. You get better.

Now your level of competition is even greater, but now you find that there are even faster swimmers than the one's you've been looking at all these years. You try to analyze their strokes, but you realize you aren't flexible enough to do that or your knees just don't bend that way. You aren't nearly that strong. You try to mimic, but everything you do is still ten times slower than anything they do. Their muscle structure is larger than yours, they're taller than you are, they have longer torsos, they have fingers and feet that are super human sized. The worst thing is, you realize that most of these swimmers, don't abide by the rules you've been taught and drilled into you for years and years. They breathe every stroke, their kick is off beat, one arm enters straight and the other bent and they pull outward instead of down. It's all fucked. Everything you've ever learned is completely fucked.

You feel like these people have made a mockery of everything you have tried to achieve or maybe the teachers have cheated you this whole time and pretended they knew best when really they knew very little. It is all an insult to your hard work and all that you have ever tried to achieve which is...??? And suddenly you realize you can't even remember what that is.

This is what life is like.

This is where I'm at.

What am I swimming for again? Where am I going? Why am I going this way?

"Wait a second, why did I do this again?"

"Oh yeah, I liked it, that's why."

"Well I liked it, then what did I do?"

"I tried to get better."

"And did I?"

"Yes, I did."

"Then what happened?"

"I'm not sure. I think I liked my teammates, I liked working out, I liked getting better, I liked winning."

"Then what happened?"

"Things became serious."

"How so?"

"I started losing. The practices got more intense, I didn't have enough rest at the walls to create bonds with my teammates, nobody laughed as much as they used to."

"But I kept trying to get better, I kept going?"

"Yes."

"Why? *WHY GODDAMNIT!*"

"You get caught up in it all. The mentality. The hope that you could still possibly become the best?"

"And why do I want to be the best?"

"I guess I don't know."

"Was that ever my goal?"

"No."

"What was?"

"To have fun. My father always told me that I never had to be the best, just one of the best."

"Why would I even want to be one of the best?"

"I don't know."

Smack. "Yes I do."

"No, I don't."

Punch. "Yes I do."

"No, I don't."

Hit your head against a wall. "Yes I do."

Fuck, stop it. "Stop it."

Break through boundaries. That wall that you hit when you can't think of anything, well think through it. That wall doesn't exist. You put it there! And you can make it disappear. SMACK. "Say it!"

"Because I wanted to be special. I wanted people to notice me and look up to me!"

"Why?"

"Because it means I exist."

"SO WHAT!"

STOP, FUCK YOU, WHAT DO YOU WANT FROM ME! "I want to be remembered for doing something great!"

"There it is! I finally said it! That might be a pretty good goal. Do I have to swim to do it?"

"I guess not. I could do something else."

"Maybe something else that I enjoy and have superhuman sized feet in?"

"Maybe..."

"Do I know what that might be?"

"I don't know."

"Well, that's okay, as long as I start looking for it. Try to find something to hold onto, and give it a shot. If it doesn't work, try again, and again, and again. All the swimming, all the practice, it was all preparation for something, but not necessarily for swimming. I can always go back, but do it for –"

"—Fun and because I like to do it."

"That's right. The original goal. I can do math, science, politics, English, history, art or whatever it is. It may not of even been invented yet. Just make sure I remember why I'm doing it, that I want to do it, and that I love to do it and that I remember *why* I'm doing it."

"Everyday? But what if I don't like the road it takes to get me there?"

"Whatever it is, I'll make my own stroke out of it. After I get everything I need, then I'll be the one setting the path. I'll be the one training the coaches and not the other way around."

"And if I die before I get there?"

"Get there. I'm still racing the clock, trying to get to the wall. I don't have forever and if I do die, at least I'll die having fun while doing what I love. Fighting is what matters."

I hear someone say that the study guide for the final will be handed out on Friday. I think it's the teacher. The word *final* seems to spark a cord as if acknowledging a finish line. It is an end to something that is painful and wearing on me. I walk out of another class dazed and feeling like I missed a whole hour and a half of my life. I need to sleep.

I hear my phone ringing. The caller ID reads a name that leaves a shocked expression on my face. Michelle, Connor's girlfriend, is calling me. I haven't spoken to either of them in a while. I know of drama from my roommate who tells me limited amounts. The rest I can see for myself with her crying all the time. I pick up the phone.

"Hello?"

"Hey, Drew?"

"Yeah, Michelle. Whats up?"

"We're friends right?"

"Huh?"

"Like you think of me as a friend, right?"

"Umm...sure." Like a mosquito sucking the life out of me, yeah sure.

"Well, I have a question. You know, how Connor has that ex girlfriend, Mandy, from high school? Do you think it would be weird if I facebook friended her?" Facebook is an online medium where one can "friend" other people, essentially anyone who is on the facebook network, which includes mostly high-school and college students.

"Are you seriously asking me this?"

"Yeah, do you think that would be bad?"

"Yeah, very bad. Why do you want to friend her anyway?"

"I don't know. I guess I wanted to find out what she's like."

"Michelle, if you start looking for things to get upset about, that's what you're going to find. Mandy is over with. He likes you. If you start digging into the past you're only going to get hurt."

"So you don't think I should?"

"No. It's stalkerish and crazy."

"Okay, I won't. Thanks Drew. You're a good friend." Friend? I fucking despise you and you should be kicked in the ovaries. Where is this coming from?

I laugh awkwardly out loud, "Okay Michelle. I'll talk to you later."

What the fuck was that about?

I get another call.

What's going on?

It's mom. She wants to know how my shoulder is doing. I find myself listening intensely to her voice, figuring in every detail, trying my hardest to retain how it sounds. I take in the amplitude, the pitch, the tone. I need to remember it. I've been saving every phone message she leaves me.

I don't know who is speaking anymore. I'm a puppet, I don't have the strength to be a Richard. I'm breaking down.

They, the ones at the funeral home, showed us how they would prepare our bodies, which machines sucked out all your organs, cleaning you out of everything that once gave you life. They only leave the outer shell like a snake skin that's been shed or a caterpillar after it turned into a butterfly. There's nothing there, but we make out like there is. They'll say goodbye to nothing. I'll say goodbye to nothing.

CHAPTER NINETEEN

I see her. Not by face, but by name. I know who she is, though she looks like another. We're all just faces and names, but feelings – to feel someone is on an entirely different level. We happen to be walking by each other, in passing, and I say hi in voiceless sound.

Her expression scares me and I can already sense it coming. She looks at me like she's never seen me before in her life or like I'm crazy. I think she thinks I'm crazy. Maybe I am crazy. I shake my head and pass it off like nothing has happened and keep walking into the parking lot where I left my car.

There are people everywhere, every day people, you and me type people, on their day to day routine like they're coming out of a supermarket. I'm comforted by them because none of them are looking at me like I'm crazy.

My tan Toyota Camry sits exactly where I left it and I can feel myself take a slight breath and my heart stops beating so fast because everything seems normal again. I beep the car open and go to the door. It's then that everything stops, like the moment before a crash, it's real, but you don't want it to be and you start making excuses for everything.

The back door window is open half way. Did I leave it open? Did someone break in? Is something stolen? My eyes start panning the back seat. Then I notice it. The trunk is popped open. Not a crack, but completely upright. I know it wasn't open before. I take a step back. The back door on the opposite side pops open, then closes just as quickly. Then the one on the same side opens then slams shut. The trunk closes. The word GHOST pops into my head. The front window starts sliding down and then the front doors start opening and swinging shut. Open, close, open, close. Every mechanical piece in the car comes alive: windows up, windows down, doors open, doors shut, the sunroof opens. Open, close, open, close.

My heart beat is escalating more, but everything is so clear. I step back further and further. Get me out. Nobody notices a thing, they just keep to their routine. Nobody even glances at me or gives me a look. Nobody sees the car. Nobody sees anything. Open, close, open, close.

A shadowy figure hangs by a noose outside my childhood window. The blinds are wide open. I always keep them shut. He sits there, hanging by his full weight blowing slightly in the night's breeze, forcing me to stare at him.

Demons crawl, mouths stretch while they string together trying to stay closed. Their bodies like black melted cheese, their eyes open and empty. I run, but they crawl and grab and yank and pull me back. I run, but they're everywhere. Black upon black, sticking to the floor, screeching and painfully crawling for hours and hours. I stop running, exhausted and admitting defeat. They circle around.

Again it all stops for a second. It's the moment before a crash and you know it's coming.

I pick up a small petri dish like the one's you see in science labs and in the middle of its black solution is a dark green face: the face of all the other demons. I pick it up and hold it close to my face as it begins screaming. One scream, two louder, three louder... Ahhhhhhh, Ahhhhhh, AHHHHHHH." It continues wailing and roaring in my ears sending my hair on end and my spine curves to the point it wants to snap. All of me, every fiber of me is awake and shaking. Scream! "AHHHHHHH! My hair feels like it's going to break out of my skin. Scream! Scream! Scream! Get me out. "AHHHHHHH!" ENOUGH!

Without even thinking about it, suddenly I find myself screaming back in the same voice of the demon, screaming back in its demon face! Screaming back at it for everything! "AHHHHHHH! AHHHHHH! AHHHHHHH! AHHHHHH!" I Scream until there's no breath left in me.

It's all out on the table. I've broken. I've given in. I suddenly realize what I've done and everything pauses again because I know it's coming. My worst nightmare about to come true and I know it's going to happen before I even see it.

Like a proud father, the green demon face turns out from its ugliness and smiles warmly at me ☺

***

I wake. Every muscle in my body is shaking uncontrollably. I'm a ticking time bomb. I need to talk to Jessica.

I get out of bed, but I don't know where to go. It takes me a second, I sit there shaking, then I remember: It's time to go to class. Which class? State and local, right. Good, now go. Okay.

I'm being pushed everywhere by an invisible hand. Maybe an invisible man. He hides in my body like a shadow I can't escape from. I find myself walking out of the way of the sun, hugging walls, trying not to be seen by anyone, but I can't hide from him.

I make it midway through class before I realize that there's no point in being there. I'm still shaking. I grab my bag, and walk out. I need to sleep, but I'm scared to sleep. I need to sleep, so I sleep. I dream frightening dreams, but they're the kind I can forget. When I wake up, I'm still shaking. I go to see Jessica. On the way, I see my professor for the class I walked out on. I try to dodge his glance, but he sees me and approaches.

"You alright?"

"Yeah, I'm *good.*"

"You ran out in a hurry this morning."

"Oh, yeah, I wasn't feeling good."

"But you're good now."

"Yeah. Sorry."

"That's okay, glad to hear you're feeling better."

I walk away.

"What does it mean?" I ask Jessica. "I think I'm losing it. I've never felt this bad before."

"Okay, we'll go over the dream, but for now I need to ask you, do you feel like hurting yourself, or have you thought about killing yourself? I just need to know."

I've thought about other people hurting me, I've thought about other people killing me. People are trying to kill me in dreams, I'm trying to kill myself in dreams. I'm not a Richard, though.

"No. No, definitely not."

"Okay, that's good. So, tell me about the dream."

I tell her.

"Don't you see, I can't win. They beat me every night. They're trying to make me bad, into one of them, and they can. I realize it now, that they can win and that scares me the most."

"Drew, wait, who can win?"

"The darkness. Evil. All of this." She stares at me, waiting for me to say more, but I don't.

"Tell me about your mom, how is she doing."

"I don't know."

"Have you spoken with her?"

"Yes, but I don't think I'm going to speak to her much more. I'm waiting for the last phone call I'll ever get from her."

"She is still cancer free, though?"

"Yes."

"Tell me about that. How is that affecting you?"

"Something's wrong. I still think she's going to...you know."

"Die?"

I pause. "Yeah."

"I'd like you to try and say that for me."

"Say what?"

"Say my mother is going to die."

I pause again. I know what she's doing, she's breaking me down even more. I'm already on the verge of collapse and she's going to do this to me now? This is what the therapists want. It's their ultimate goal. I'm on the verge of crying. I hold back the tears. Fuck tears. "I know this all seems ridiculous. She's not dying anymore, but something's wrong. I think it's her. The connection maybe. I'm picking up what's going on with her."

"Can you say more about that?"

"The bond. I told you about it. She set it up when I was a baby. Maybe it doesn't even exist and I'm imagining it, but they say mother's have instincts about their children, can it go the other way around?" She's silent again, which is my cue to go on. "It's like a rope that's attached to the two of us. We're still tied together on the rope, but I can feel her getting further and further away. It's killing me, and probably her too, because there's only so much rope that exists. It's going to break." She gives me another quizzical look. "The strain of the rope now is becoming unbearable. I don't know how else to explain it." She's silent, reflective with her blue eyes still staring at me. "I don't know what to do. I'm afraid to sleep. All these dreams, it's like they're really happening. I wake up and it's like they're still going on. Sometimes I can't even distinguish the two. I'm dreaming up homework assignments that don't exist. I handed in an assignment the other day that my professor had never even mentioned. I completely made it up. I'll think one of my friends said something that they never said and they're beginning to look at me strangely. I'm finding it better if I just don't talk as much."

"Have you been taking the medicine?"

"Yes, and I've been sober for three weeks now."

"Is that true?"

No, it's not. I had a few drinks here and there, but pretty much nothing. "Yeah, I swear and it's still not working."

"We can up the dosage to one half, twice a day now. We can see if that helps."

"Okay."

"Are you, okay?" I'm zoning out again; I can't focus on anything for more than a few seconds.

"Huh?"

"Are you okay?"

"Yeah, yeah, I'm fine."

A long silence ensues. I stare out the window and look down at the kids going to their classes. The red bricked path with grass on the outside that looks crisp from the cold. The sun's warmth shines on me through the glass, heating up my body, and giving me strength. I close my eyes to try and take it all in. I can hear my breath slowing down, I can smell the mixture of purple and red colors from the carpet that was just vacuumed that morning. I still feel the edginess creeping under my skin, the creepy crawler bugs, but I breath, and it settles a little. I can feel Jessica staring at me with her bright blue eyes that I want to dive into. I want to swim inside her so she'll feel me too. I want her to feel everything I am and free me and help me to let go and float away in the blue of her watery eyes with that warm sun shining down. I hear the tic of the clock on the wall behind me. I see golden grass and cherry blossoms from the Botanical Garden. I hear Jessica inhale.

"What are you thinking?"

My eyes open, and I see those blue eyes have a tinge of fear in them. The darkness, like a cold breeze has gone through her like I made the mental leap inside her and she's trying her best to hide it, but I know her now. It doesn't take me long to break through all the barriers and see her as human with shadows of her own. The electricity is making her hair stand out a little and the corner of her lips are trembling ever so slightly. Her usual flat hand that rests on the arm of the chair is loosely clenched. She's so strong, but everyone has their limits, and I'm so sorry for doing this to her, for making her feel.

"I was making sure I wasn't still dreaming."

She nods her head a little, which means she's not going to say anything. She's waiting for me, and the silence makes me anxious.

"I'm not sure if I am or not, but sleeping seems worse than this now. I'm afraid to close my eyes. Have you ever been afraid to close your eyes?"

She smiles a little at this, "We're not talking about me, remember?"

"I know, but, I was just wondering and I guess maybe I just don't want to say what I'm actually thinking."

"And what is that?"

"When I was a kid, I used to take two magnets and see how close I could get them to one another without having them touch. You try to pull them away from each other while some other force is pulling them closer together. The closer you get, the harder it is to keep them from closing together. Does that make sense?"

She nods her head.

"I guess what I'm getting at is, that the magnets are really close together now, and no matter what I do, they're going to touch."

"And what does that mean?"

You know what that means. "You know what that means."

"I want to hear you say it."

"Why?" I know why.

"You know why."

I feel the fog. It's a mist that hangs over and turns everything into a swamp making it hard to move. It's what the chief talked about in *One Flew Over the Cuckoo's Nest*. I never understood it until now, but you don't see the way normal people do, it's all glazed over with something that you can't put your finger on. A fog is the best word for it, because everything moves in shades, mixes of colors and shadows. Nothing is definitive. There are no actual shapes, it all gets more and more blurred. It's all moving like looking through the glass of a washing machine. You can't make out anything except the colors of the clothes, and you can't take your eyes off of it because it's mesmerizing.

All the teachers, the coaches, and your friends, their words are lost to the background of that churning color. It's like a permanent day dream, the more I sink into it, my vision no longer seems true to itself and it's as if I'm watching somebody else watching me, watch the washer and nothing is really happening at all. The colors are falling further away into the background. People are becoming less distinctive. Then I'm falling into the background. I'm the voyeur, or the ghost, or maybe I'm already dead. This is how my mom is feeling. I know this, because this is not just me. We're tied together with a power she put into place long ago. A force that she understands and I don't. I'm watching through her eyes, feeling more and more of what she is because it's getting stronger. Like a frequency she's the main radio tower and I'm only picking up static, but the stronger the signal the more I can make out of what she's feeling like a million voices screaming out in unison from a terrible tragedy. I can hear these things because she hears them. Dying is making her that much more powerful.

She's morphing like the caterpillar to the butterfly. She's changing from the tower to becoming part of the frequency itself. The doctors won't be able to understand why the morphine they give her doesn't help and why she will still be crying out in pain. It's because it's not just her pain she's feeling now, it's everyone's. She can feel mine, my father's, all of her friends, the people in hospital beds near by, all in that giant washing machine, hitting her all at once. Making sense of things is no longer possible until it's over. "She's dying." I tell Jessica. "My mom is definitely dying and it's too late to do anything else to help her."

CHAPTER TWENTY

"Are you ready?"

Huh?

"Are you ready?"

"Ready for what?"

"I'm not talking to you." Josh looks over at me from his side of the room. The clutter, the obnoxious posters on the wall, the not knowing what's going on, it's all getting to me.

"Oh...sorry."

"Tina, how long does it take you to get ready? Let's go."

"I don't wanna go." She's standing in front of the mirror putting an earring in. She gives Josh a look of disgust.

"Why not?"

"Ugh." Tina storms out of the room.

"What did I do?" Josh says to me.

"Huh?"

"Oh my god, forget it." He stands up and walks to the door.

"What's going on?"

"I'll tell you later. Michelle's pissing everyone off."

"Oh...What'd she do?"

"I told you, I'll tell you later. Just relax, and don't say anything about it."

"Okay." He leaves and I'm alone and curious so I get up to follow, but they rush back in, nearly knocking me over.

"Oh, sorry dude."

"I just don't want to go, okay?" Tina goes back to putting her earrings in.

"Why not? Just ignore her."

"Josh, could you just shut up!"

"What are you yelling at me for?"

"Errrr." She stomps her heels on the ground.

"Relax!"

She walks a couple of steps to where Josh is sitting on his bed, and she gives him a small kick in the shin, and walks out again.

"Owe. Are you kidding me?" Josh laughs. "My girlfriend's nuts." He whispers to me half jokingly.

I shrug my shoulders. He stands up and goes after her again. I stand up and go after them again.

I see Tina crying, while walking out of the building with Connor behind her and Josh behind him.

What's going on? I walk next door to Connor's room where Michelle is. I knock, and hear her voice tell me to come in. I figure she says she's my friend and I hate her now for stealing my friend, but maybe she'll tell me her side of things and our relationship will get better again. Maybe there is still a chance to reconcile everything and it be like it used to be when we were all friends and we didn't keep secrets from each other. I have to try and see whether or not she can be a human being. I need to give things a last try. I haven't had an opportunity to talk with her yet, this seems like a good opening. She's lying down on a top bunk, calmly reading a book.

"What'd you do?" The words come out more accusatory than I wanted them to, but I don't want her to know that Tina is upset, I just want to find out what happened.

"Me?"

"Yeah." I say more softly.

"I didn't do anything."

"You sure?"

"Yeah, I've just been sitting here reading."

"Oh, okay," I say and smile, "Never mind then... Sorry." I close the door, feeling a little awkward. Maybe I should have mentioned Tina or anything about how I feel, but her response shut me up. If something happened to make her upset, Michelle would have known what I was talking about, right? Maybe I should mind my own business, but I just can't help it to want Connor back even though my contempt for him is skyrocketing. I want one last chance. I want one last chance at everything, one last chance for the fake world to make sense to me and for me to be accepted into it. I need him back like I need mom back.

I go back to the room. The anxiety is building as nighttime approaches. It knows sleep is coming and it's getting ready for

another night of insanity. I hear the outside door open and slam shut.
I hear the stomping of steps. I feel jittery. I hear another door open
and close, then I hear crying. I go outside the room and see Tina
crying with Josh sitting on the common room couch. I go over, and
try to comfort her as well.

"You okay?"

Sniff, "Yeah." She gives me a hug.

"Is it okay if I sit or do you want to be alone?"

"No, it's okay."

I tell Josh that I tried saying something to Michelle.

"What'd you do that for?"

"I wanted to see if I could help the situation."

"You're a fucking idiot, now Connor's going to be pissed."

"I know it was. I feel like I'm being left out of everything now
a days and you guys are all running around not telling me anything."

"I told you I'd tell you later."

"Yeah, but – "

I know it's my fault. I know I fucked up, but I'm sick of
being patient. I'm sick of waiting for things to go back to the way
they were. I'm sick of being Drew. I want to be Richard. I want to
shake the glass and move things my way for once, but whenever I try,
everything goes to shit. I see Connor come out of his room like a
raging animal let out of the gates of the Coliseum.

"Did you talk to Michelle?" His breath is heavy and wavering. I see his nostrils flare, and his eyes are dark, yet glazed over with a fiery anger.

"Yeah," I say, with a sudden confidence building in me, and I don't know why or where it's coming from. I find that I've stopped shaking. I think it's because I want to die, but maybe it's because it's the first words he's said to me in months and I'm happy to at least hear his voice directed at me. Even if it's like this, at least something is happening.

"I don't know what you said to her, but you ever make her cry again like that, and I swear I'll kick your fucking ass."

I laugh. "She's crying? Really?"

This pisses him off even more so that he turns and goes back into his room.

My laughter turns to seriousness. He won't even hear my side anymore. It's just her. Dori was right all along. He'll take a girl over his best friends. I'm trying so hard not to give up on him, on me, and he's rejecting me on every front. Doesn't he get it? I can see myself as him if I didn't know about my mother's abilities. I'd have his faith in trying to hold on, I would have blue eyes, I would have a girl who I could run to all day and hide away from the miseries of the world. He'll dismiss us all for a girl he's been with for less than six months and I don't want him to turn out like that because he's better than that. With his faith and my knowing, we could battle cancer back into the black hole in which it came from because we'd challenge the world into the ground. I'd give up and he would tell me not to. He would hold on and I would tell him when it is time to let go, but now we just hate each other. We've fueled the cancer instead of healing it. It is one thing if he left, ran away with the girl he only thinks he loves and never looked back, but he's here. He's in my face every day, knowing what he knows about my situation, and not caring about anyone except himself. This was never the Connor I knew. Now, I hate him. That other side of me is dead. Hope is dead. I say it out loud.

"I hate him." I stand up. "I hate him." My voice gets louder. "I fucking hate him." I mean I hate the world, I hate everything. I hate him. "I fucking hate him." I grab a nearby chair. I'm the psychopath in the mental hospital. I'm the guy on PCP that you just can't stop and mom's smile is nowhere to be seen. I see Josh out of the corner of my eye try to come up behind me to stop me, but he backs off as I lift the chair high into the air and crash it down onto the wall. "I fucking hate him!" I bring the chair down again splintering it into pieces, denting the wall. I hear his door open.

Connor comes at me fast and pushes me back against the wall. I drop the chair and smile my Richard smile.

"What's your problem, man." He says and pushes me again. We fly into my room.

"You! You're my problem!" His face is raging, and I'm aware of everything: the intensity, my heart beating through my chest, and my anxiety finally feeling free to unleash itself.

He pushes me again and raises his fists. I'm so happy I could fly. I want him to pound me into oblivion. "Hit me!" I want the bugs to burst out of my skin. "Hit me, goddamnit!" He's backing me into a corner. Put my head through the wall and let me swim in the brain matter I'll never have to deal with again. "Hit me!" No more dreams, let me fucking feel something. I stop. No more fear, no nothing. Clean, black...Death. Give it to me. "HIT ME!!!!"

Silence. His one hand grabbing my shirt, his other fist raised, I hear his heavy breathing start to slow and his face loosens up, followed by his fist, and he let's go of me. He turns around and walks out of the room without another word. After he's gone, I watch as several heads peer into the doorway from both sides. One of them speaks.

"Drew?"

The room seems quiet and still. It's the shock.

"Yeah?"

"Anybody ever tell you, you are one scary mother fucker."

CHAPTER TWENTY-ONE

There's something about Connor coming back and apologizing. I think I make him admit it too. I make him admit to taking a girl over his best friend and there's no denying. He takes the rap, admits to everything, and says that we'll talk about it at a later time that will never come. I hear Dori's voice. She says she's going to come visit mom and I at the hospital. I tell her she doesn't have to, but she says she wants to. I tell her I could use the company. I tell her she's the only one. She tells me she loves me and I tell her I love her, and I tell her thank you. There's lots of darkness, intoxication, limbs flying everywhere, breasts on top of me, climaxes I can't even feel, swirls of light, movies that never end, silence's that sound blissful, and all the school facts I can never retain.

I say hi to doctor Seuss under a trufula tree, then climb onto an elephant, who brings me to a beach with two young naked girls wearing sunglasses. They giggle at me. I jump off the elephant and watch as my own clothes disappear. I lay down to talk to them, then I'm tickling one of them and then I'm inside the black world of nothing till they get up and we run into the sea. The sun is glimmering off the water creating patches of white glare. It's one of those pictures you draw when you're little, except this one has naked girls.

I jump into cool water to come out standing with a gun pointed at my head. The face of an older man with a beard turns to the young face of Richard who never really died. He laughs at me like he always does. I run and he fires. The gun just keeps firing, and I just keep running. I'm in one of those movies where the bullets fly in every direction and the good guy never gets hit. There's a park with my grandfather playing chess with another older man. The older man sees my grandfather look up at me, he turns around and his face is as black as burnt bread. There are pieces of flesh hanging off and only a small patch of still pale skin remains. He opens his mouth wide and I'm sucked into it: tilt up, dolly in, snap zoom.

There are pink walls like angled off mountains with a camera in the middle spinning. The camera bursts into flames. Darkness falls and a bunch of middle aged men and women are gathered around a campfire. They are all holding hands with their eyes closed. I sit down to join them. They don't like that though, and they all open their eyes at the same time, which are a fiery red. They turn their heads toward me and I hear them scream a high-pitched scream that tears through my spine like a spinning saw. There's more blackness as I walk through one of the main hallways of my middle school. There are rows of lockers and a tiled floor. A small light with no source shines on a lone girl I once had a crush on. She's sitting down bent over her knees, small, and scared. I feel myself getting smaller and tears come to my eyes. I'm a little kid again. Her head turns to mine and her eyes are filled with tears too. I sit down next to her. She rests her head on my shoulder and I close my eyes to feel her there so close to me. It's there that I can melt away.

Footsteps make their way across the hall. We look up to see her girl friends making a disgusted face at me. They point and yell something in sounds I can't hear, but fully understand. I watch her look at me, one last look, before she gets up and runs away with her friends. I stand up, sad, but knowing that it would come. A figure I know as myself makes its way up a spiral staircase tiled in black and white. It goes up, but the stairs move down. Up and up and up it goes, but the figure never moves at all. A Frisbee flies through the air over a dog running to catch it. He's big and brown with a smile on his face as he comes back all proud with the Frisbee leaning out the side of his lightly drooled over mouth. I kneel down to rub his head before grabbing the Frisbee and throwing it off again.

I hear clanking.

My spine knows before I know, that cold shiver like an icy stream coming over my back, and I don't want to turn. I look down at the ground, the blackness fading in, the tears forming again in steady eyes. I want to run, but I'm too tired to care. I'm shaking so badly now. She's shaking so badly now.

I hear metal clanking louder.

The ground quakes and I know exactly where to turn. The hardest thing in the world is just to turn. My legs are shaking, and my fingertips dangle trying to feel their way out of the dark fabric of space. There are no more excuses. My hands are frozen and the earth has grabbed me with its grass soldiers who whisper to me through the moving air.

Clank. Grinding metal. Sparks. Turn.

Hahahahahaha.

Turn.

I turn, slow, real slow, but it seems so fast. I look up into a bathroom mirror through which the metal puppet with the face of a forgotten Disney character holds up a small buzz saw in one hand and my decapitated head in his other. Sparks fly. I stare into his plastic face with its plastered on smile. Its blue eyes with exaggerated lashes are open wide, innocent and friendly. He looks at me, then looks at my head in his hands, then back at me. Everything's mechanical.

He reaches his hand into my open neck and yanks out my brain, which squirms around in his hand like a live jellyfish. It drops from his hand onto the ground, and makes its way toward me on the veins that were once connected to my neck. It scuttles toward me, fast, like a red tarantula and gets onto my foot. I start kicking and screaming as it makes its way quickly up my leg and onto my stomach. I try brushing it off with my hands, smacking at it as hard as I can, but it dodges my every swat. I can feel it on my stomach. I can feel it making its way up. I can feel it squirming all around. I don't want to look. I can't look. Wake up, please! Wake up! WAKE UP!

I jump up sweating, not knowing where I am. I see dad is over to my left in the bed next to mine. The place is symmetrical: there's a television on the other wall in between the two beds surrounded by a wood cabinet made for its shape, a small night stand exists on the same side of each bed with a lamp on it, there are flowery curtains over a window, the air is stale and chilled, two emerald green chairs laced in shadows face inward to each other at the other end of the room, and the sheets are tight around me with four pillows under my head. We must be in a hotel room, though I don't remember how we got here.

I sit up staring at all the shadows who want to attack me, but they slowly recede as my eyes focus. They are still moving so fast that I can see them jumping around, turning into different shapes, but as soon as I focus in on them they go back to the way they are truly set in the room. I know I'm awake because of that smell of a room left with the Air Conditioner on all day. Dad's loud snoring overwhelms my still rapid breathing and the drone of the air conditioner overhead. Memory fades back in and I remember that mom is dying. Dad is here to take me home to see her. I know as much as you do about what's going on. The semester is over, but I didn't finish. We both know what's coming.

I know I'm not going back to sleep anytime soon so I go into the bathroom to rinse water over my face. The light from the bathroom is blinding enough to wake me up and I'm glad that my eyes can finally focus on something other than shadowy monsters.

The bathroom has that typical hotel mirror that covers the entire wall with a glassy reflection that is your ultimate judge. I let the sink run after rinsing my face several times and just listen. No songs blasting constantly through my head, no thoughts, just the sound of running water washing away the dream. I listen as all the little droplets fall through the small black hole on their way to being recycled through the planet. "Someone will feel this," I think to myself. The water will eventually find its way to the surface. A thousand screaming voices can be heard by someone a million miles away, like a tidal wave can make its way around the Earth. Our screaming is getting louder, because there is only so much we can take. We will be heard; we need help. It shouldn't be this way. As much as we try to ignore it, our arms are shaking where they are bent over the flat porcelain of the sink. I feel her shutter as I start lifting. my head to stare at my own reflection. She jolts, and I suppress it. She screams no, and I scream we have to. We're done resisting, she says no we're not. My head lifting slowly up, finally meets its own gaze. Behind that cold glass is a pair of gray eyes, focused in and conceding to everything that is evil. A black devil in the image of a tall hooded man with a black-crusted smile stands passively behind my reflection. The rest of his face hides behind the darkness of his own existence, but that plagued smile is meant to be seen.

He is the shadow of the past six months. He is my creation. He is my mind of darkness unleashed of its own free will and finally taking form. His giant hand is on my shoulder with long stretched out fingers, wilted like my grandfathers, but black as the sands of cursed beaches. Those nails, like the extended threads of a great God who can pluck the fruit from a tree or scratch out a life like an impetuous cat.

I can feel him. His smell is like the remains of burnt flesh forgotten in a chilly hospital bed, dried out and untouched for a long time, but I can feel him. It all comes across as sweet honey and an end to a long insatiable thirst. In those black eyes I can't see, but I feel the suppressing weight of a never-ending dream like a river of consciousness where I finally decide which way the current flows.

Standing there like the impregnable statue that he is, still, yet all suspecting, his dry repulsive lips form a word that he doesn't mouth. It is that one word that I hate so much. I can't escape from it. "Good" he says, and that's all. He stands erect and glowing in a world that is fading away behind the mirror. I feel the hatred growing inside me with him encouraging me. I feel like a young boy ready to lash out hatred onto the world. I want to scream and rant. I remember how it felt to throw that chair against the wall, I remember the faces of young boys whose faces I punched in when I was younger, I picture all the teachers who I've wanted to strangle over the years and I see myself strangling them. I recall all the news of murder, crime, and hatred and decide it's easier to stop fighting against it and stop being afraid and just become a part of it. You can't fear the monster when you are the monster.

Richard had it right all along. He's dead, and I'm still here. He died winning all along until that quick loss when his head smashed its way through a tree. I see those dark green eyes grow an even darker gray and more focused than ever before, knowing truly what the world is, knowing that you can't escape, knowing that it is easier to give in, knowing that mom's cries are undeserved, but nobody really cares or they would stop it. My entire body is shaking now. It wants this, but she's holding me back. Torn between too many worlds and her. I lift my arm up to go to punch the glass and shatter us both to pieces, but I know before I even do it, what will happen. He'll laugh, a deep pretentious laugh and that will be it. Nothing will be solved. It's like killing myself in the dream. It won't make the darkness go away. I lower my hand. Torn between worlds, yet I can still feel her power over me as the strongest of them all. It suddenly dawns on me why I am the way I am and why I'm not Richard and why I can never become Richard. She's given it to me and I hear her finally say, "yes" and through the darkness, I can feel her smile.

The grey eyes un-focus. They turn back from grey to a light green. The shaking stops, and my muscles loosen. I smile only a half smile, a friendly one, at the shadow behind me and his smile disappears. I take my weight off my arms and stand as erect as he is, then I close my eyes. He releases his hand from my shoulder, his head tilts in puzzlement, and his nails fold back into his dark sleeve. I feel mom's hand in mine. I hold it as her whole body shakes constantly in the hospital bed. I tell her it's going to be okay, and I say goodbye. I tell her thank you, and I say goodbye. I tell her I love her, and I say goodbye. I imagine my shadow disappearing and so it does, taking in the glass of the mirror into the blackness, taking all the bone chilling laughter, all the screaming, all the pain…and Mom.

Mom passed away one week later, the dreams stopped as soon as she did. She suffered immensely in that week, moaning and convulsing even through high levels of morphine. But as I said, it's okay. I get to see her more now than I ever did before. She visits me in my dreams, not always looking the way she used to, but she's happy there. We take walks along a brown dirt path surrounded by apple trees and there's no rush or fear— no sense of time. We have forever to just walk and talk. We talk about everything and sometimes we don't talk at all. There's a stonewall we like to sit on and watch the sunrise amongst a world that we created. Colors so vibrant you can feel them across your skin and when you look up, all you see are sprays of purple and a mix of oranges that blanket the sky. There's nothing to stop us. She's there when I'm awake; I can *feel* her there. It's not how I imagined it to be. I still remember me as a little boy sitting on a carpet playing cards with her. Dad sometimes regrets, telling me, "There are things I wish I could have said." And I have to remind him that she knows. She's known all along. We're the ones who need to know now. All we need to do is believe her. That's what she's tried to tell everyone all her life. I finally did, and now, everything's *good,* really good.

THE END

AFTERWARD

I realize now, that sometimes the best place to start is at the end.

Mom had passed away and Dad and I were left in the House. I
remember thinking of it that way too, recollecting the name only as
'The House', no longer 'Home' – just a place we had both lived for
twenty years with her – left to look at walls that we flooded with
memories, left to pick up silver wear that shined back with her
reflection, left with closets filled with clothes that still smelt like her –
it was hard not to economize the good and bad that swirled in our
minds, to weigh them out upon each other and try to make the good
memories win.

You know, to make us happy again.

But the good seemed far away and the bad all around us.
Out of nowhere, sitting on a guestroom bed together, no longer
wanting to feel estranged in our own home, I smile up at dad.

"Let's take a vacation."
For six years, friend after friend had asked us, 'Let's go here, let's go
there…we're going on a cruise, want to come?'

You swallow hard. You remember. 'No,' you say mechanically, this
line you've rehearsed through repetition with lots of excuses, sorry's, I
cant's, maybe next times, and as you say all these things your words
have sentences behind them that beg them, that plead with them,
'please, please, please don't ask me why' – and of course, they always
ask why.

What was so hard about a simple question? Because If they asked
that, then you would have to admit to yourself that something was
wrong and that your life was different from everyone else's, you
would have to admit that she was sick and that she could die, you
would have to return to that place in your mind where your decisions

and your life didn't truly belong to you and so your response back would both be a lie to them - and worse - a lie to yourself. Any vacation was spent with her, or not too far from her, or the *guilt* of not being with her, so it didn't matter what we did, we realized we hadn't enjoyed ourselves in six years.

As soon as I asked dad, "Let's take a vacation", he smiled too, because he knew what I really meant. "Let's fucking enjoy ourselves".

I'm sure to anyone else this would seem disrespectful to Mom's memory. I think some people have this idea that your are *supposed* to suffer and that there is this mourning period that everyone must take and that it has to go a specific length of time to be deemed socially acceptable. Well, personally, and I really mean this in the best way possible – I think those people are nuts.

This is why, when only a few months later, Dad started dating one of mom's best friends – and only two years later – got married to her, I wasn't upset. It was funny, because everyone else was upset. People who had no understanding or no involvement in our lives judged my father for his actions while I was happy for him. Family members turned their noses up at him, friend's voices gave their judgments away and it became ironic to the point of hilarity. We were the ones who suffered and they were the ones who were supposed to tell us exactly *how* we were to suffer and live our lives from then on.

"Where would we go?" Dad turned and asked and even the sound of his voice had a smile that told me he was entertaining the idea.

The answer was obvious, "*Anywhere*", but I continued, "And by that I mean preferably someplace with sun, beaches, and beautiful women."

"Okay," Dad said still smiling, "When?"

"*Now*" but I continued, "And by that I mean probably something like Wednesday so we can pack our bags and not have to pay so much for the air fare."

There was a pause, but dad nodded excitedly in a way that made it look like his whole body was nodding up and down on the bed. "Okay!"

We packed our bags and we were off two days later to a little island called "St. Thomas". It was filled with sun scorched water, teal beaches you see only in postcards, and beautiful women.

Still only twenty and the drinking age being 18 in St.Thomas – I had a little too much fun.

It was on the flight home that I began thinking about mom again. The after-effects of the alcohol was giving me clarity and I heard the words of the psychiatrist telling me how my alcohol use was part of my depression and I wondered if I even needed alcohol in this way anymore. The whole week was spent trying to squeeze the last remnants of mom out of my mind, but then looking out the window of the plane, relaxed and comfortable with the sight of the water below, I was ready to remember.

The plane – and it crashing into that beautiful water below – became a metaphor for the journey I had with mom's illness.

The plane had finally crashed, I was still alive, and the water was still beautiful.

This was something I had to come to terms with, and this is why at the end of my book I say that everything is "good". It is a combination of the irony of how everyone says, "I'm good" when you ask them how they are doing - even when they don't mean it - and the reality of my present feelings towards the world – which is the truth – It is good, and maybe I mean, it is good to be here, and maybe by that I mean, it is so good that I want to live even in the absence of my mother.

I wrote this book the year after she died. It became the reverse of my alcohol. It was my chance to remember her rather than to forget.

I am 28 now, writing this 'afterward' to see where the world has taken me since that time in my life and to share what has happened since.

My roommate Josh, is now married. We had his bachelor party down in New Orleans and had the group get back together for a great time. He has fulfilled his dreams of travelling and is now living with his wife out in California. I still miss him a great deal and we stay in touch here and there.

Connor still likes cars. He is the manager of an auto-body shop and is doing well for himself. He eventually got back with Dori and two years later he broke up with Dori. He is now with the girl Dori was first upset with him about. The girl he had 'cheated' with that Dori had initially broken up with him about and that had almost caused his suicide – it all comes full circle. She is his childhood friend and they are very good together and I 'think' he is happy, but it isn't always easy to tell with Connor.

I have lost touch with Dori over the years. She graduated law school and after her break up with Connor, she fell out of touch with our group and no one has really heard from her since.

Kat, our swim coach, has since retired and our old assistant coach is now head of the swim program – as it should be.

My dad got re-married to a wonderful woman who is a college professor. She even helped me to edit this book. Before my mother had died, she had whispered into my father's ear, "Don't worry, you will always have Alice" and that is who he is now married to.

As for me, it has taken me many years to stop living for other people. Living with mom's illness had prevented me from thinking about my own desires for so long that I think I never learned how to follow my own heart and mind. I moved back to NY to be close to my father for some time, but am now trying to follow my own dreams and have moved to Florida. I am only a few miles from the beach where I nearly died at 2 years-old, and I think that despite that experience, I loved that day and the beach and the warm weather and it has brought me back here. I am still writing, though life has taken me in so many directions that I think I was waiting to have more to write about and hope to have another book finished by the end of next year. Before mom died she told me that I would have a daughter, one of the last of her many predictions. I'm looking forward to when that day comes.

My mom now rests in the Catskill Mountains in New York in her favorite pond that we visited often as I was growing up. She called it 'The frog pond' and it is covered in beautiful lilies, painted turtles, and of course frogs who sing to each other at night beneath a sky loaded with stars. Before she died she gave me a children's book that she wanted me to read after she passed called, "The Little Prince". It took me years to even open it.

In the story, I think she is the Little Prince and I am her friend who helps her to find a spring of fresh water in the middle of a desert.

At the end of the story, The Little Prince is going home to his star somewhere far away. He says to his friend, "At night, you'll look up at the stars. It's too small where I live, for me to show you where my star is. It's better that way. My star will be...one of the stars, for you. So you'll like looking at all of them. They'll all be your friends. And besides, I have a present for you." He laughed again.

His friend responds, "Ah, little fellow, little fellow, I love hearing that laugh!"

"That'll be my present. Just that…It'll be the same as for the water."

"What do you mean?"

"People have stars, but they aren't the same. For travelers, the stars are guides. For other people, they're nothing but tiny lights. And for still others, for scholars, they're problems. For my businessman, they were gold. But all those stars are silent stars. You, though, you'll have stars like nobody else."

"What do you mean?"

"When you look up at the sky at night, since I'll be living on one of them, since I'll be laughing on one of them, for you it'll be as if all the stars are laughing. You'll have stars that can laugh! And when you're consoled (everyone eventually is consoled), you'll be glad you've known me. You'll always be my friend. You'll feel like laughing with me. And you'll open your window sometimes just for the fun of it…And your friends will be amazed to see you laughing while you're looking up at the sky. Then you'll tell them, 'Yes, it's the stars; they always make me laugh!' And they'll think you're crazy. It'll be a nasty trick I played on you…And it'll be as if I had given you, instead of stars, a lot of tiny bells that know how to laugh."

"I won't leave you" says his friend.

The Prince says, "It'll look as if I'm suffering. It'll look a little as if I'm dying. It'll look that way. Don't come to see that; it's not worth the trouble. You understand. It's too far. I can't take this body with me. It's too heavy…But it'll be like an old abandoned shell. There's nothing sad about an old shell…And it'll be fun! You'll have five-hundred million little bells; I'll have five-hundred millions springs of freshwater."

She gave me this book and I'm glad I read it. As difficult as it was. Now, whenever I look up at the stars, I have five-hundred million things to remember about her and laugh, and wherever she is, out on one of those stars, I hope she is looking out and seeing five-hundred million things that remind her of me.

Made in the USA
Middletown, DE
05 November 2017